# Monksfield

# Monksfield

Jonathan Powell

Foreword by Brough Scott

World's Work Ltd

Copyright © 1980 by Jonathan Powell
Published by
World's Work Ltd
The Windmill Press
Kingswood, Tadworth, Surrey
Set, printed and bound in Great Britain by
Fakenham Press Limited,
Fakenham, Norfolk

# Contents

# Acknowledgements

The story of Monksfield could not have been completed without the co-operation of those closest to him. Des and Helen McDonogh in particular were unfailingly helpful during my long stay at Billywood. Warmly hospitable, they provided me with endless background material and answered my more absurd questions with amused resignation. Their friendly support was invaluable.

Tommy Kinane and Dessie Hughes, with their families, made me instantly welcome in their homes. Both men talked frankly about their part in the tale and both emphasized the enormous pleasure they had gained from riding Monksfield regularly.

Arthur and Peter Ryan helped me piece together Monksfield's early days and Dr Michael Mangan and his wife Sheila, on a visit to England, helped enthusiastically with essential detail and interesting anecdotes.

My thanks also to Pip Pocock for checking the detailed veterinary terms, to Colm Farren for his generous assistance, and to Sarah Reeves for accepting so cheerfully the task of translating my scribbling into type.

There are many others who have made invaluable contributions to the preparation of this book. My grateful thanks to them all for giving up their time to discuss the character and personality of the horse they admire.

6

# Foreword
# by Brough Scott

Horse biographies have two obvious but screamingly crucial problems. Their subjects are only of a child's age and do not even have a toddler's vocabulary. They would make Boswell shut up his notebook and run.

So the interest of the books depend significantly on the people surrounding the four-legged hero. It also helps if like Monksfield and all National Hunt horses he has done a bit more than just win a couple of classic races and hobble off to the sultan's life at stud when all of 3 years old.

Racing of course is the iceberg sport. Only 10 per cent of the story, the bit on the racecourse, is above the waterline. What most people knew about Monksfield off the track could be written on the back of a betting slip. But Jonathan Powell's instinct for a story has for long made anteaters look a bit snub nosed, and he has rooted out such a cast of characters that you start suspecting he might have been at the bottle.

Well, would you believe that Monksfield's breeder is the world's greatest authority on moon landings? That his trainer previously starred in Charley's Aunt? That his regular jockey once knocked out on the club circuit 500 people a week? Or that the horse himself only survived his darkest hour after a visit from the local witch doctor?

In fact if you think for a minute, you will soon start believing. For Monksfield is a story from deepest Ireland and Jonathan Powell has come up with so much authentic magic and names like McNamee, McCabe and naturally McGuinness that you almost end up with a hangover.

7

But all the flavour, all the characters still couldn't pull a story like this together unless the horse at the centre was a bona fide hero. With Monksfield there was never very much doubt. Even the visible tip of the iceberg part he has always been much more than just another champion hurdler. The little colt with the swinging front leg, the big brave eye and the almost tangible will to win had soon become a symbol of the soaring athletic courage that can lift racing far above mere animated roulette.

I know no racing picture that more perfectly captures these qualities than that of Monksfield jumping the last flight in the 1978 Champion Hurdle. Looking at it again reminds me how moved I was watching this little horse battle triumphantly up the Cheltenham Hill, and surely the ability to excite the spectator is the ultimate test of the great horse.

But if a great horse can thrill people from afar, he is a source of hand-warming wonder to those closest to him. It may seem odd to some cynics that at this corner of the twentieth century we might be attributing quite such qualities to a horse. But these pages show just how much happiness, affection and even anguish one little horse can bring.

I had never believed that within six years a book could appear to match the glorious colourful record breaking story of Red Rum. I was mistaken. Read now about Monksfield and his people and see why.

# I

# The Duel

The sustained duel between Monksfield and Sea Pigeon in March 1979, in driving rain and deep clinging mud, was the most enthralling finish ever seen on Cheltenham Hill in the 52-year history of the Champion Hurdle. Eight other horses paraded with them beforehand, but they were relegated to the role of bit players as the two principal actors were locked together in combat over the final 3 furlongs.

Monksfield, the reigning champion, was still, most unusually, an entire horse, a small, rugged individual with a strange galloping action, an indomitable spirit and a magnificent head. Bred virtually by mischance, rejected at the yearling sales, he had been spotted and bought cheaply by a youthful former office clerk. Just starting life as a trainer, the young man relied on instinct and flair to guide his new purchase to the very peak of achievement in racing.

Sea Pigeon, his challenger, was much larger, handsome, almost black, a relentless racing machine tuned to perfection over the years by three different masters of the training profession. Classically bred in America, owned initially by a multi-millionaire, Sea Pigeon had been precocious enough to win a valuable race at Ascot as a 2-year-old and possessed sufficient natural talent to finish close behind the placed horses in the 1973 Derby. Bought shortly afterwards as a potential hurdler for what bloodstock agents describe coyly as a five figure sum, Sea Pigeon had become a more enthusiastic warrior after a gelding operation.

The pair had finished first and second in the 1978 Champion

Hurdle and had dominated the hurdling scene ever since. Now they were thrown together on the same battleground in appalling conditions to settle arguments that had been raging ever since their last meeting.

Hunched alone in the jockeys' changing room at Cheltenham Monksfield's regular rider, who had recently been displaced in painful circumstances, watched the race forlornly on television, his ageing, lined face etched with sorrow. Thousands of miles away in Arabia Monksfield's young breeder twiddled in vain with his hired car's radio to tune into the race on the World Service programme.

At Cheltenham, racing out into the country on the very wide outside Monksfield was tracked by the seasoned campaigner Beacon Light, the brilliant young prospect Kybo, and Sea Pigeon, while a second larger group chose the shorter but muddier route on their inside. Jumping boldly and accurately Monksfield stole half a length at several flights and a fine leap at the hurdle at the top of the hill gained further ground.

His doting trainer Des McDonogh, watched nervously alongside Monksfield's owner. The strain for both men, half-way through the race, was almost unbearable. Des McDonogh recalls, "The crowd around us started to roar when Monkey threw that great 'lep' at the top of the hill. I turned round to the boys and begged them to give him a chance, and the next thing I'm shouting louder than any of them. I couldn't control my excitement any more."

Now the race began in earnest. Dessie Hughes, the Champion's jockey had dictated the pace throughout, setting a good even gallop, but if he was to blunt Sea Pigeon's speed the moment had come to call on Monksfield's inexhaustible supply of stamina and courage. Quickening down the incline he soared over the second last hurdle in a clear lead. Close behind him Kybo, trying to match strides, failed to rise high enough, clipped the top bar and crumpled on landing.

One danger had evaporated but another much more potent threat materialized for, as Monksfield struggled through the quagmire towards the final bend, Sea Pigeon, making ground rapidly and absolutely cantering, arrived on his inside. To those of us in the stands it seemed the decisive move of the race, and

10

Jonjo O'Neill his jockey was convinced he was about to win the Champion Hurdle at last. He confirms, "I was *sure* Sea Pigeon would win. I would have preferred to sit a bit longer behind but my orders had been to take him on before the last. So I let my fellow stride on perhaps half a length into the lead and I was going so easy it was just unbelievable. I didn't feel anything. I was just smiling."

Dessie Hughes, aware of the challenge, felt Monksfield tighten under him. "He gathered himself together, got down to it and raced. You could almost feel him thinking he was not going to be beaten. He just changed into another gear and stuck his head down lower and lower. I've never ridden a horse to go so fast into a hurdle in my life. We were both flying."

Sprinting into the last hurdle Sea Pigeon still held a half length advantage. Jonjo O'Neill could be seen crouched motionless holding his mount together for the final thrust up the finishing hill. He reports, "All I wanted was for Sea Pigeon to pick up at the right time at the last hurdle and I knew I must win. Three paces off I saw a lovely long stride, my horse stretched at it, came up right, and I thought that's it, Monksfield's got to make a mistake if he tries to come with us."

Six months later the surprise was still in Jonjo O'Neill's voice as he added in dismay, "My lad jumped it perfectly but Monksfield picked up with us and actually gained as he landed beside us. I didn't think it was possible. He was so far off it that at the speed we were travelling any other horse would have run straight through the hurdle. Yet he *gained* on me. I couldn't understand it. It was against all nature. As he takes off he must have such a spring in him, like a gazelle."

Dessie Hughes confirms, "I gave Monksfield three smacks before the last hurdle and he met it spot on, went into it faster than Sea Pigeon, and landed back in with a chance, even though Jonjo was going to beat me for the first 50 yards after the hurdle."

Certainly the photographs taken at the final flight of hurdles reflect a marked contrast in attitudes between the jockeys. Jonjo O'Neill, smiling broadly, is sitting still with the proverbial double handful. Dessie Hughes, teeth clenched, his eyes hooded in concentration is caught wielding the whip powerfully in his

11

right hand, asking for a final supreme effort.

For twenty, perhaps thirty tingling strides the two combatants raced up the hill locked together. At first Jonjo O'Neill was still confident of victory. "I thought he was bound to die, but he kept coming back at me. I could sense him gritting his teeth, and then that *awful* moment, I could feel my lad weakening. I really asked Sea Pigeon and he gave me *everything* but all the time I could see Monksfield's head coming and my fellow was going empty, his strength ebbing away."

Beside him Dessie Hughes' furious driving finish was helping Monksfield to inch alongside his great rival. "Once we were level I knew we would win. He had me beat from the time he headed me but as soon as I joined him again I had him beat. The stride that I got to him proved it because he did not come with me for the second stride."

Monksfield stormed into the lead, his game little head held so low he was almost brushing the mud as he strained to reach the line first. Beside him Jonjo O'Neill changed from a confident victor to an anxious uncertain competitor. Turning his whip over in his right hand he gave Sea Pigeon three hard cracks, but I doubt if a grenade exploding at his quarters would have lifted him past Monksfield. So they ran to the line, the extraordinary champion and the best horse never to claim that title. At the post Monksfield had won by three-quarters of a length and way back far more than the official verdict of 15 lengths Beacon Light staggered into third place.

Months later Dessie Hughes felt able to describe the horse that had won the most stimulating duel ever seen on Cheltenham's hill. He says, "People love a horse with a big heart and they don't come any bigger than Monksfield's. It's unbelievable how much a horse will give you if he is willing. Monksfield gave me his last breath, his last ounce, every single bit he had left. He ran his heart out, and offered it without complaining. I'm probably harder with the whip than some jockeys; I don't know it at the time but I realize it later when I watch a race again on television."

"I never felt I was hard on Monksfield. He behaved like a man of a horse. He took all I gave him and did not squirm from it. I think he needed the assistance. The other horse was going so easily the task was more than he could manage on his own."

12

Jonjo O'Neill recalls, "I was sure I had won the race until the last 100 yards and then I had to hit Sea Pigeon. I had nothing to lose. I hit him two or three slaps and there was nothing there and all the time Monksfield kept going. It was the gamest race Sea Pigeon has ever run and my only bad luck was to meet Monksfield. Even when I congratulated Dessie afterwards I couldn't believe I had been beaten. I have nightmares about Monksfield at Cheltenham. He must be the gamest horse there has ever been in training. I never knew a horse could be so genuine, so tough, and after more than sixty races over five years. It should be impossible. He loves racing, he has that extra bit of zest. The tougher the task you give him the harder he will try and you will *never* beat him, because he's so determined, so honest, so gutsy, something jockeys dream about."

# 2

# The Fluke

All form and reference books state that Monksfield was bred in Ireland. You could be forgiven for assuming that his breeder also lives there, a farmer perhaps, with green rolling acres and an instinctive knowledge of racing. Nothing could be further from the truth.

Monksfield's breeder Peter Ryan, fresh faced and articulate, is an expert on outer space who lives in a cramped two-roomed flat squeezed between the Kings Road and the Fulham Road in the shadow of Stamford Bridge, the home of Chelsea Football Club. Peter Ryan had never been to a bloodstock sale until the day he bought Monksfield's dam Regina, has not attended one since and was only there to meet his cousin Arthur Ryan. It was a monumental coincidence that took Peter Ryan to Dublin that day and a decade later he is still pleasantly bemused at the chain of events that led him to breed such a courageous and popular champion.

Born and educated in Yorkshire, the second son of an Irish father, he is a writer, who, at the time he bought Regina had only the vaguest interest in racing and was planning a book on the expected first landing on the moon the following year. Peter Ryan's link with Ireland, where so many of his relations still live, was re-established when he spent five years at Trinity College, Dublin, by the ruse of switching courses half-way through.

Sitting in his favourite pub, Finch's, "It has all the best characteristics of an Irish bar," in the Fulham Road, dressed in blue jeans and open necked shirt, he explains, "I was bored with reading chemistry and one night was in a pub in Dublin with some friends when we spotted the Professor of Irish and the Professor of Geology. I explained my dilemma and over a few pints of Guinness the Professor of Geology invited me to his lecture the following morning. I found it a fascinating subject and decided to change from chemistry."

Like most students he was short of money at University. Peter and his friends either drank or ate, and often relied on Guinness which seemed to take care of both functions. His attempt to open an account with the then Royal Bank of Ireland in Foster Place in his first days at Trinity left him with a warm respect for the ways of the Irish.

He recalls, "The manager asked if I was a student. I nodded. He then asked what I was studying. I told him chemistry, and he felt that would not look very good on the forms and suggested I put down economics. He asked if I had a grant. I nodded again. He asked if the cheque had arrived. I shook my head bleakly."

The manager continued, "Then you'll be requiring a small advance, won't you?" Thus Peter Ryan opened his bank account with an overdraft.

Occasionally Peter and a few friends would head for Naas races, south-west of Dublin. Once three of them pooled their resources, backed a 14/1 winner and eased back to Dublin in a haze of Guinness and champagne to take their girlfriends to dinner at the best restaurant in town.

"That", says Peter Ryan, with emphasis, "was the first time I was aware of the financial embraces of racing."

While at Trinity he wrote for the University magazine and once penned a 2,000 word epic for the *Irish Times* for which he was paid £4. He was dimly aware of the bloodstock sales a few miles away at Ballsbridge, but had not the slightest inclination to go there because, as he says, "In those days £10 was a huge sum of money and the idea of people spending hundreds of thousands of pounds on racehorses seemed absurd."

During his stay in Ireland he took the opportunity one December weekend to visit his cousin Arthur, whose family had lived and farmed at Inch, five miles from Thurles, in County Tipperary, for 500 years. There's nothing colder than a large Irish country house, without central heating, in the middle of winter . . . and Peter resolved to plan his trips at a more agreeable time of year. Once he returned to Inch in the winter, with snow on the ground, to find the front door wedged wide open in the hope that the January sunshine might warm up the chilly house. He walked inside, looking for the family, and as he peeped round the door of the dining-room a large mouse scurried out of a turkey carcase resting on a meat dish on the mantelpiece.

Soon after Peter Ryan completed his mammoth spell at Trinity with a degree in Geology and a passionate interest in space, he spotted an advertisement in the *Listener* seeking recruits for the new BBC 2 television channel. At the subsequent interview his science degree proved a major asset and he got a job as a researcher at Television Centre. It was an interesting enough role backstage but Peter had other ambitions. However his first faltering attempt as a front man on television proved disastrous. He remembers shaking and stuttering awkwardly on a pilot science programme. Later he was interviewed by Kenneth Allsop on the '24 Hours' programme and asked to explain a replica of a lunar rocket but his hands were so shaky that he had difficulty putting the simple model back together in one piece.

After two years he left the BBC early in 1968 to start a fresh career as a freelance broadcaster working mainly for Irish radio in London. That summer he proposed a book on the expected first landing on the moon the following year. The idea was rejected, but he determined to use his savings to go to the United States for more research on the book in the belief that his publisher would change his mind.

Peter Ryan had been working as a freelance for seven or eight months when he was invited by Radio Telefis Eireann to their Donnybrook studios in Dublin to discuss a more permanent and lucrative role with them. What better opportunity to see Arthur Ryan and his family again? He rang Arthur a few days before the trip, saying he would be in Dublin on November 12th 1968, and was thinking of travelling down to Inch for a brief stay.

"I can save you a journey," replied Arthur. "I'm hoping to buy a brood mare at the Goffs sales in Dublin on the 12th and 13th so why don't we meet there." The sales complex at Ballsbridge was just over a mile or so from RTE's offices. Peter Ryan completed his business there in mid-morning then wandered along to Ballsbridge to find Arthur Ryan and his wife

Arthur and Elizabeth Ryan at the Ballsbridge Sales on the day Regina was bought.      *Credit: Peter Ryan*

Elizabeth leaning over a rail chatting with several friends. Always careful with his money Arthur Ryan had bought a mare, Rising Song, cheaply at Goffs the previous year for 150 guineas and was hoping to find another bargain. Peter Ryan watched intrigued as Arthur Ryan and his friends studied various mares, spotting faults, highlighting good points. Arthur was interested in several lots but he had only £600 to spend and they all made too much money.

The constant talk of mares and foals began to stir Peter Ryan's imagination. Fascinated by the atmosphere at Ballsbridge that day Peter began to think that he, too, might like to own a broodmare. He had some money in the bank and, totally unaware of such matters, believed that if you bought a mare in foal, then the sale of that foal a few months later would cover your expenditure and probably leave you with a profit.

He recalls, "The idea occurred to me that instead of leaving the money I had saved in the bank and gradually spending it, somehow or other I could be involved in this breeding business. Yet that had been the last thing on my mind when I met Arthur. As the project crystallized in my mind I thought in terms of sharing a mare with Arthur in joint ownership, but he said it would be better if I bought the mare and he looked after her as I had the money and he had the facilities."

Peter decided he could afford to spend up to £1,700 so after flicking through the catalogue the two men set off on a lightning inspection of likely mares. After looking hurriedly at a dozen possible candidates their choice fell on an 11-year-old mare Regina, bred impeccably, a failure on the racecourse, but certified in foal to a modest stallion, Dual.

Says Peter, "I had an instinctive feeling about this particular one. There was certainly no carefully considered decision. It happened in the way sometimes you make a decision and it's correct, even though you can't explain why. I think I had an intuitive feeling, her breeding was good and Arthur backed me up."

Arthur Ryan remembers the moment differently. He insists, "Peter would not know which end of a horse comes first and his sudden decision to buy a mare surprised me. I think he wanted to go back to his smart friends in Chelsea and say he was a racehorse breeder. It would give him a talking point and he had the money available."

Arthur continued, "Regina caught my eye. She was certified in foal. I did not know an awful lot about bloodlines at the time. Until then I'd been more interested in breeding hunters, show horses and half-breds. But even I could see she had a fine pedigree."

What Arthur Ryan failed to realize was that Regina had produced one foal in the six previous years. Had he known that vital fact Arthur Ryan would not have bought Regina even though she was in foal again at the time of the sale.

He says, "I had no chance of checking her breeding record before, probably because there was not enough time. Had I done

Peter Ryan poses triumphantly with Regina moments
after buying her for 1,500 guineas at Ballsbridge.
*Credit: Arthur Ryan*

so I certainly would not have been interested in buying her. The
catalogue did not mention the fact. Catalogues don't tend to
carry the bad things ... but I would notice it now."

Arthur Ryan had heard of Regina's sire Tulyar. He remembered him winning the Derby. He knew nothing about Dual and
was unaware of Regina's poor breeding record. The choice at
that late stage of the sale was limited so the decision was taken to
try for her. Arthur volunteered to do the bidding with Peter
whispering encouragement at his shoulder.

The bidding opened at 700 guineas, Arthur Ryan came in at
800 guineas and stayed in until faltering briefly at 1,200 guineas

in the face of determined opposition. He's a man with a reputation for holding on to his own money and now he felt anxious
at splashing out any more of his cousin's.

Peter, in an excited state of knowing he wanted something
badly yet close to his limit, motioned his cousin to continue
bidding until he stopped nudging him. A few moments later
Peter Ryan was the new owner of Regina at 1,500 guineas.

Peter was triumphant. "The motive in buying her was instinctive. Being an Irishman living in England it gave me a kind of
identity to have a horse there. It also put the money out of my
reach. I felt it was a risky but interesting investment." He laughs
at the memory of that heady day. "It was a pure fluke that I was
there but I've never regretted it."

Only later did the young writer and broadcaster appreciate the
high quality of his new mare's ancestors. Breeding can be a
mysterious subject. When odd matings occasionally achieve a
successful result, breeders will spend hours explaining how
astutely they planned the whole thing. The truth is that the
whole business of breeding thoroughbred racehorses is a huge
gamble. Some readers may find the whole topic of breeding
eternally dull yet Regina's background illustrates just how in-
efficient and infertile she had been at stud until she produced
such a famous champion. Regina was bred in the purple from the
very best lines built up over many years by the Aga Khan, the
extent of whose vast bloodstock empire may be gauged by the
fact that he was leading owner no less than thirteen times
between 1924 and 1952, and leading breeder nine times.

Regina's sire Tulyar had won the 1952 Derby and her dam
Tambara won several top class races, including the Coronation
Stakes and was second in the 1,000 Guineas, the first of the fillies
classics at Newmarket. Her dam Theresina won three important
races, including the Irish Oaks and Falmouth Stakes and apart
from Tambara produced seven other individual winners. These
included Turkhan, successful in the St Leger, Irish Derby and
second in the Derby, and Ujiji, third in the Derby, winner of a
wartime Gold Cup, and subsequently a sire of steeplechase
winners.

Theresina had, in turn, been bred by Teresina, one of the Aga
Khan's foundation mares, bought for him by the brilliant trainer

George Lambton for the near record price of 7,700 guineas in 1921, the year that the Aga came into racing. Teresina was trained by Dick Dawson and as a 3-year-old finished third in the Oaks, second in the Coronation Stakes and Eclipse Stakes, won the Great Yorkshire Stakes, and completed a hectic season by running third in the St Leger and second in the Cesarewitch. A thorough stayer, the next year she won the Royal Plate, Goodwood Cup and Jockey Club Cup and is remembered by Bob Lyle in his book 'The Aga Khan's horses', published in 1938, as one of the gamest and finest stayers ever seen on an English racecourse.

Lyle describes her 1924 Jockey Club Stakes victory over the previous year's Derby winner Papyrus in glowing terms.

"Papyrus forced himself into the lead and it seemed that he must win. But if Teresina was somewhat deficient in speed there was never any question of her stamina and courage. Fighting on with wonderful pluck she caught Papyrus just before the winning post. A fairer exhibition of courage no horse could have given."

Over half a century later her great-great-grandson Monksfield inspired the racing world repeatedly with that same appealing blend of determination, stamina and downright refusal to accept defeat.

Regina's breeding was immaculate, but she proved a disappointment when put into training in France with Alec Head, who had twice suffered a narrow defeat in the Champion Hurdle. In 1947 Alec, riding Le Paillon, was beaten by just a length by National Spirit and had to face a hostile reception from the crowd on his return. Le Paillon surely gained a unique consolation for that defeat when he won the Prix de l'Arc de Triomphe in Paris seven months later. That was Alec's only ride in the Champion Hurdle, but four years later he trained Pyrrhus to finish second to Hatton's Grace in the race.

Alec enjoyed no success at all with Regina. Small, with an attractive head, she was an unconsidered outsider on the only three occasions she ran in 1960. Eighth was the best position she managed in any of them. She failed dismally to live up to her considerable family reputation and was entered in the end of year clearing sales run by Tattersalls at Newmarket.

21

Her excellent pedigree and neat good looks caught the eye that day in December 1960 of Sir Harold Wernher, an experienced racehorse breeder and owner, whose wife Lady Zia later owned the 1966 Derby winner Charlottown. Regina was knocked down to Sir Harold for 4,000 guineas, expensive enough for such a disappointing filly, and she was taken the few hundred yards to his Someries Stud on the edge of the town. Sir Harold hoped and believed that Regina, like many well bred fillies before her, would succeed in passing on the talent at stud that she had failed to show on the racecourse.

But after an initial bright start, when she bred a Persian Gulf filly foal named Georgia at the first attempt in 1962, later sold for 510 guineas, she proved stubbornly incapable of conceiving another foal.

Regina's visits to Alycidon in 1963, Crepello in 1964 and 1965 and Kelly in 1966, all proved fruitless. She spent part of those years at the Wernhers' Blackhall Stud near Naas in Ireland. A broodmare with the best pedigree in the world is of no use to a stud if she is infertile, so after four barren years the Wernhers decided to cut their losses and sell Regina. She was visiting the Blackhall Stud at the time so was entered in the Goffs November sale, 1965, at Ballsbridge.

Bloodstock values fluctuate sharply. In 1960 she had been worth 4,000 guineas. Now she was sold for a paltry 120 guineas to Bertie Kerr, the eldest of four brothers, shrewd and astute, a man who combined owning and breeding racehorses with running the family bloodstock business Kerr & Co which he established in 1920.

Bertie Kerr, who died in November, 1973, told his brother Desmond that he had been attracted by Regina's fabulous pedigree and he predicted that one day she would breed a classic winner. At the time Kerr also owned a promising stallion, Dual, who curiously enough had been bred at the Someries Stud. Dual was the obvious choice for Regina's first mating under her new ownership and it proved a success, for in 1967 she produced a filly foal named Dual Queen, who won as a 2-year-old, was sold for 8,000 guineas at Newmarket in 1971 and whose foal subsequently proved a champion in Spain.

Unfortunately for Kerr, Regina reverted to her former style

22

and proved barren when he sent her back to Dual. He persevered, tried a third mating between Regina and Dual the following spring in 1968, and gained his reward when she was duly declared in foal. Two years in foal out of three is by no means a bad record for a mare at stud but in the autumn the decision was taken to enter Regina in the Goffs sales.

Desmond Kerr, now managing director of Kerr & Co, can scarcely keep the regret from his voice as he recalls, "The man in charge of our entries department put her in that sale partly because she was a shy breeder and difficult to get in foal. I remember clearly that my brother Bertie did not want to sell her but he allowed himself to be persuaded against his better judgement. Afterwards he was very annoyed at letting her go."

So Regina found herself in the sales ring at Ballsbridge, on November 12th 1968, and was sold for 1,500 guineas to 28-year-old Peter Ryan.

Arthur Ryan returned to Ballsbridge the following day and after much debate bought for himself Gay Exposure, a fine, big mare, for 600 guineas.

# 3

# The bargain
# everyone missed

Arthur Ryan agreed to board Regina for his young cousin. The deal was straightforward enough. Peter would own the mare and pay the stallion and vets' fees. Arthur would take care of the stud fees, look after Regina and the two men would share her produce equally. The agreement was scribbled down at the sales on the day Regina was bought and witnessed with a signature over an Irish stamp.

So Regina moved to a new home at Inch, a sprawling 350-acre farm, whose long drive has more holes than an aertex vest. Arthur and Elizabeth Ryan live with their five children in a large, shambling, in parts crumbling Georgian manor, built in 1700 on oak piles driven into rabbit sand. It's a draughty old building, with enormous windows, a relic of another age and you can appreciate why, in the winter, the Ryan family spend much of their time huddled in the tiny kitchen.

Arthur Ryan, a trained engineer, runs a machinery business and is also a hard working dairy farmer but the efficiency of the operation is certainly not reflected in the appalling clutter of papers, desks, letters, typewriters, magazines, files and old newspaper cuttings that cover every inch of his spacious study. Tall and sparely built, his thinning grey hair swept back from his prominent forehead, Ryan has a slightly doleful expression and prefers action to paper-work. He was master of the local pack of foxhounds for a while, ran the Holy Cross Beagles for sixteen seasons and, until recently, spent several summer weekends roaring round Ireland and elsewhere as a rally driver.

He rode his second point-to-point winner in 1974, at the age of

55, a little matter of 22 years after his first one, and now takes an occasional day off to pursue his new hobbies, flying and sailing.

Arthur Ryan milks seventy dairy cows and keeps a similar number of young cattle, calves and bullocks, some of them grazing alongside as many as twenty horses, a mixture of hunters, half-breds, ponies, mares and yearlings. Regina and Gay Exposure joined them late in 1968 and both foaled safely the following spring. Gay Exposure proved infertile afterwards and was finally sold at a loss.

Within weeks of the birth of Regina's foal Penguin Books contacted Peter Ryan in May 1969, to confirm they would like him to write his book on the first landing on the moon which was expected imminently. Peter had already written the first and last chapters, on the history and the future. During the historic flight in July, between blast-off from Florida to splash-down in the Pacific Ocean ten days later, he wrote an astonishing 90,000 words with the help of data sent back from the American Space Agency, NASA, and the astronauts' dialogue, wired to him verbatim.

Ten days later his record of the landing by Neil Armstrong and his two companions was on the bookstalls. The book eventually sold 175,000 copies in the English language and many thousands more in several other languages. He has since written four children's books and a major work on the solar system which are on sale in both England and the United States.

Regina's foal, called Dindon, was sold as a yearling for 650 guineas and won £6,000 in prize money in Greece. The Greek equivalent of *The Sporting Life* must be one of the few periodicals not gathering dust in Arthur Ryan's study so news of Dindon's triumphs did not filter through to Inch until much later.

The Ryans' first choice as a new mate for Regina was Hardicanute. Says Arthur, "He was a high-class racehorse and had won over £30,000 in prize money when they were pounds and not the little bits of paper we have now."

Safely in foal, Regina returned to a 35-acre field at Inch, close to the house and adjoining the drive, with abundant green grass and excellent shelter under beech and lime trees. In due course she produced another colt foal, Horik, sold to trainer Richard Carver outside the sales ring for 800 guineas as a yearling.

Arthur Ryan on his last point-to-point winner Mistral perched on the front door of his home Inch.

*Credit: Peter Ryan*

Arthur Ryan recalls, "Both Dindon and Horik were far superior in looks to Monksfield. They were thicker, more substantial. Horik was especially good looking with a lovely action, which was a bit surprising as Regina's action was terrible when she cantered round the field." Horik, too, did well on the racecourse, winning six races in France. Once again news of foreign success took time to reach Inch.

In London Peter Ryan was pleased with his investment. In touch by telephone and letter with his cousin, he made sporadic visits to Ireland and was kept informed of developments. His half share of the proceeds of the sales of Dindon and Horik had brought in a reasonable return on his capital and he agreed that Regina should return to Hardicanute. Their rematch produced a filly foal, Athalia. A note in Arthur Ryan's breeding file reports that her hocks were not 100 per cent at birth.

Arthur recalls, "The hocks soon came right. Athalia was a beautiful looking foal, the best that Regina produced. She had everything going for her."

At the yearling sales Athalia was knocked down for 3,000 guineas to George Rogers, a noted judge of breeding, bidding for Tim Rootes. Peter Ryan was delighted at the price when he rang Arthur that evening.

George Rogers, kind, wise and elderly, had spent years breaking in, educating and making young horses for the redoubtable Miss Dorothy Paget. Now he was training on his own and was also on the look-out for likely prospects as brood mares. He knew all about Regina's ancestry.

"The most marvellous female line of all, you know ... The best family in the Stud Book, she traces back to Blue Tit," he assured me, his voice suddenly serious. Then a twinkle came into his eye as he added, "but that's long before your time and almost before mine."

All George's considerable skills as a trainer failed to galvanize Athalia into speedy action. In despair after four poor runs he put her in a modest maiden at Mallow. She trailed in at the back. Finally she ran in an upside down handicap at Limerick Junction carrying a postage stamp of 7 stone, 2 pounds. In a field of ten she beat two. While George was pondering Athalia's fate shortly afterwards an Australian woman rang to ask if the filly was for sale.

"Would you take £15,000 for her," she inquired casually as Rogers recovered from the shock at the other end of the telephone. The female philanthropist from Down Under arrived the next day, looked at Athalia and paid up without a murmur.

But while Athalia's birth was imminent and Horik had not yet run, Peter and Arthur Ryan were once again settling down to the delicate task of selecting a stallion for Regina. She had produced two foals in succession and was about to have another one, a considerable improvement on her early days at stud.

Peter Ryan explains how the choice was made. "I would be in Ireland often enough to pop down to Inch. Arthur would do the research and recommend two or three alternative stallions. He would tell me what he thought about them, then we would have a discussion and select one."

Racing is littered with ifs. If Arthur Ryan had realized Regina had such a poor breeding record he would not have bought her in the first place. If he and Peter had known Horik would be such a useful racehorse they would have set their heights higher with Regina's subsequent matings. Now a third visit to Hardicanute was ruled out because his conscientious stud groom Tony Butler, who had taken endless trouble with Regina on her two visits, had moved to another stud.

A friend Percy Harris, a local breeder, mentioned a new stallion recently arrived from America, Gala Performance. He was reasonably cheap at £300 and, most conveniently, was standing nearby at Coolmore. He was also a big horse, another asset.

Arthur explains, "At that stage all Regina's progeny had been a bit small so we wanted to increase the size. I went to see him and liked him. He looked straight and level with good bone. Peter and I talked it over and decided to send Regina to him. But if we had known how good Horik was going to turn out we would have sent Regina to a better, more expensive stallion."

Gala Performance, born in 1964, had been a tough, durable horse in America, winning nine of his thirty races over two seasons. He won four Stakes races at 3 years and had been second to Damascus, the best 3-year-old of his generation.

The man responsible for bringing him to Ireland was Tim Vigors who in his early days insisted on being described as a horse dealer. In the late 1960s the reputation of American horses was not so high in Europe as it is now. Tim Vigors was one of the first to realize that their horses were as good if not better than their European counterparts and had the foresight to buy Gala Performance for syndication in Ireland.

Gala Performance was a big, powerfully built brown horse, a high-class son of the brilliant Native Dancer. He arrived in England late in the spring of 1968, covered a handful of mares at Newmarket early in the summer, then moved to Coolmore in County Tipperary, for his first full season the following year.

Regina, heavily in foal, was sent to the Coolmore Stud in May 1971. Arthur Ryan's records show she foaled Athalia there on May 24th, was covered by Gala Performance on June 1st and 3rd, again on June 28th and 30th and came home on July 4th. She spent the summer with the usual mixed gathering of hunters,

# Gala Performance

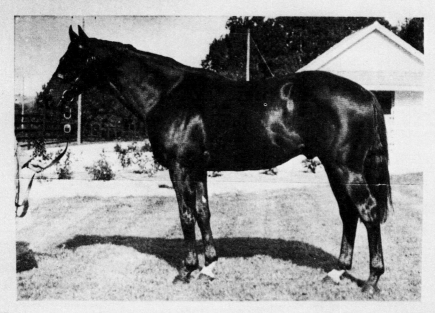

(Brown horse, 1964, 16.1½ hands)

**ISIS**

**Standing at COOLMORE**

| Age | Starts | 1st | 2nd | 3rd | Earnings |
|---|---|---|---|---|---|
| 2 | 11 | 3 | 1 | 4 | $ 13,849 |
| 3 | 19 | 6 | 4 | 3 | $130,006 |
| Total | 30 | 9 | 5 | 7 | $143,855 |

**GALA PERFORMANCE** pedigree:

| | | | |
|---|---|---|---|
| Native Dancer (gr, 1950) | Polynesian | Unbreakable | Sickle / Blue Glass |
| | | Black Polly | Polymelian / Black Queen |
| | Geisha | Discovery | Display / Ariadne |
| | | Miyako | John P. Grier / La Chica |
| Red Letter Day (b, 1952) | Rosemont | The Porter | Sweep / Ballet Girl |
| | | Garden Rose | Colin / Garden of Allah |
| | Good Example | Pilate | Friar Rock / Herodias |
| | | Parade Girl | Display / Panoply |

Four of **GALA PERFORMANCE's 9** victories were gained in Stakes events. At 2 years, he won 3 races, and was placed 5 times from 11 starts. At 3 years, he won 6 races, including 4 Stakes races, at distances of 1 mile or over, the most valuable of them being the *Jim Dandy Stakes, Saratoga*, 1 mile (beating **Bold Hour** and **Tumiga**); also finished 2nd in *$100,000 Wood Memorial Stakes* (to **Damascus**).

By the brilliant racehorse and sire, NATIVE DANCER.

Out of RED LETTER DAY (won 3 races at 2 years), **GALA PERFORMANCE** is own-brother to *RING AROUND* (Maryland Derby), and half-brother to *SCARLET LETTER* (dam of *Cold Comfort*, one of the leading racemares in America); their grandam GOOD EXAMPLE bred 6 winners, and is the second dam of the Stakes-winners **Exclusive Nashua** ($132,029), **Irvkup** ($112,508), **Exclusive Native** ($169,013), **Mellow Marsh** ($83,000), **Prince Papule** ($40,033), **Clover Lane** ($113,000 at 2 years), and **Fleet Discovery** ($30,025). Due to his late arrival from America in the middle of the 1969 covering season he had only seven 2-year-olds in training. Up to the middle of October, six of these 2-year-olds had run and 3 are winners and 2 had been placed.

### SYNDICATED

*Enquiries to:* **Tim Vigors, Coolmore, Fethard, Co. Tipperary. Telephone: Fethard 144.**

SR 43

Gala Performance.

half-breds, ponies and bullocks in her favourite field at Inch. At the time an unusual note appeared in Arthur Ryan's stud book alongside Regina's name. 'Allergic to donkeys.' Normally a good natured mare, she would not allow a donkey in the same enormous field. At the merest sight or sound of a donkey, she would disappear to the other end of the pasture and stand snorting angrily for up to half an hour.

Arthur Ryan believes in rearing his animals and his family to be tough. Regina stayed out until winter's frosty fingers made their chilly imprint on the field where she grazed and was then brought into a large, draughty box in the untidy yard behind the house. In the colder evenings she was given a light rug. Whatever the weather the large top door on her box was always left open. Sometimes in the bitter cold Elizabeth Ryan would steal out at night to the yard to close the top door.

As the spring of 1972 merged into early summer it became clear Regina was going to foal rather late. Remembering her late mating with Gala Performance Arthur and Peter Ryan decided

Lismacue Stud where Monksfield was born.

*Credit: Peter Ryan*

not to send her to a stallion and so miss a year. Arthur intones mournfully, "It's expensive to miss a year but she was so late."

Anxious that Regina should have the best attention at foaling time Arthur Ryan sent her on May 31st to the nearby Lismacue Stud to be under the eye of his close friend William Barker, an experienced vet. On June 7th 1972, Regina produced a healthy colt foal with pretty markings, a hardy little individual, much later to be named Monksfield.

Two days later mother and foal travelled the few miles back to Inch. They spent the summer out to grass. Arthur Ryan was not exactly impressed with the new arrival.

"He did not have the quality of her previous foals", he says, "and later, as he began to trot and gambol around the field I spotted his appalling action. At a walk, of course, his movement did not show up too badly. But he had a terrible action when he started to go faster. We call it winding, as his two front legs go out and round in a great big circle."

In October the little foal was weaned from his mother. He wintered well enough. Lightly built, rather lean, with a curious action, his best feature by far was his beautiful, aristocratic head, with bold eyes set wide apart and a splash of white down the front of his face. Peter Ryan, paying an unscheduled visit, remembers his cousin leading round the new arrival, by then a yearling, on a head collar, harping on his bad points.

"By then", says Peter, "I had covered my original investment and had learned a lot. I resigned myself that this particular foal was not going to make much money because Arthur warned me and he was a bit small and had a funny action."

Even so neither of them can have been prepared for the shock that followed at the Goffs September sales at Ballsbridge. The two men decided on a reserve of 1,500 guineas. Arthur Ryan, careful as ever, had spotted that breeders were allowed a reserve of up to that figure without paying commission if the horse was withdrawn. Regina's yearling, as we have said, was born very late on June 7th and it cannot have helped his cause to be sandwiched between much older yearlings.

George Rogers, who had bought Regina's last foal Athalia the previous year, was one of the few to inspect her latest produce in his box outside the sales ring. George kept coming back to

31

filly in Two-year-old Free Handicap of 1958, winner of three races including Gimcrack Stakes and Champagne Stakes and Emancipation, won two races, dam of winners including Spree, won two races at two years, and at three years won Nassau Stakes, Goodwood, second in One Thousand Guineas and Oaks, and dam of four winners), and Sunright (dam of Jamaican Chief, winner of 5½ races, and Zanzara, winner of four races, £3,475, including Acorn Stakes, Epsom, and herself dam of winners, including Matatina, five races, £10,805, and Showdown, six races, £23,678, including Coventry Stakes, and Queen Anne Stakes).

**Stabled in Box 207.**

**ABOUT 10.30 A.M.** The Property of Messrs. A. G. and P. C. Ryan.

**Lot 608.**

| | | Native Dancer | Polynesian |
| | | | Geisha |
| | Gala Performance | | Rosemont |
| | (U.S.A.) 10 | Red Letter Day | Good Example |
| **BAY COLT** | (Br. 1964) | | |
| (Foaled 7th June, | | Tulyar | Tehran |
| 1972) | | | Neocracy |
| | Regina 6 | | Nasrullah |
| | (B. 1957) | Tambara | Theresina |

REGINA was only lightly raced in France at three years. Her first produce, a filly by Persian Gulf, was sent to Peru. Dam of **Dual Queen** (by Dual, winner at two years, 1969, and retired to stud) and **Dindon** (by Dual, at two and three years, in Greece, in 1971 and 1972, value £2,737) also Horik (placed in France at two and three years, 1972–'73).

TAMBARA won Rous Memorial Stakes, Newmarket; Clearwell Stakes, Newmarket; Coronation Stakes, Ascot, and £5,658, also placed second in One Thousand Guineas, and Princess Elizabeth Stakes, Epsom, and third in Princess Margaret Stakes, Ascot, and Falmouth Stakes, Newmarket; dam of the **winners Princess Yasmin** (dead-heated for Prix de Saint Firmin, her only race at two years, and winner in France at three years, and placed, including second in Ebbisham Stakes, 1959, dam of winners including White Star, won three races in France at two and three years, 1965 and 1966, including Prix de Guiche, and placed second in Prix Jean Prat, Longchamp), **Télémaque** (three races, in France and placed third in Prix Daru, Longchamp, and second in Craven Stakes, Epsom), **Pakistan II** (two races in England in 1962, and placed in France at two and three years, 1960 and 1961), **Révolté** (at three years, 1964, in France), **Tazeen** (placed in France at two years, 1968 including third in Prix Yacowlef, Deauville, and winner and placed in France in 1969) and **Nadara** (at three years, 1973 in France); also Regina (see above), Korynthia (placed in France) and Distillate (sire in U.S.A.).

THERESINA won three races, £4,163, including Irish Oaks and Falmouth Stakes, also dam of nine **winners Turkhan** (three races, including St. Leger, Irish Derby, Coventry Stakes, Ascot, also second in Derby, and sire of winners), Ujiji (eight races, including Gold Cup; also third in Derby, sire of winners), **Shahali** (three races, £6,334, Chesham Stakes, Ascot; Imperial Produce Stakes, Kempton Park, and Criterion Stakes, Newmarket), **Eboo** (Rous Memorial Stakes), **Byculla** (in India), **Nemrod II** (Diomed Stakes, Epsom, and two other races), **Tambara** (see above), **Ponte Tresa** (also dam of a winner), also Benaner, Gandria, and Sirdaree (all dams of winners). Tracing to **Blue Tit.**

**Stabled in Box 208.** 493

Sales catalogue entry of the unamed Monksfield on the day he was led out unsold.

Monksfield's box and asking for him to be led out and trotted up and down.

Sir Peter Nugent, experienced and authoritative, was on the rostrum to sell lot number 608. Without so much as drawing breath he read out Regina's impressive pedigree in his deep, stern voice.

Goffs keep tapes of all such sales in case of dispute or error. It's an admirable habit that can save authors endless research.

Sir Peter began, "A very well bred colt here by Gala Perform-ance. Where will you start me for him? Give me 3,500 for him. Well 3,000. Whose got 3,000 for this fellow? Put him in then at 2,500, 2,000, yes," his powerful voice booms.

"Who has got 2,000 for him? Well put him in at 1,500 then. A half-brother to three winners," he adds in despair. "1,500, yes, well start me at 1,000."

"1,000? 800 I'm bid, at 800, 800, 820, 840, 900, 940, 980, 980 I'm bid, have you a thousand? At 980 guineas. 1,000 I'm bid, at 1,050 for him now. Any left for him at 1,050? Are you going to let this fellow go at 1,050," he pleads.

"1,100, 1,150, at 1,200, at 1,200, a half-brother to three win-ners including Horik. Any more for him at 1,200? Any more anywhere? Bid if you want him. You're going to lose this fellow, you know. At 1,200. Any more? Bid if you want him," he barks, his voice rapidly losing patience.

"Your last chance", he sounds bored now, "at 1,200 guineas. Are you done? Bidding at 1,200 guineas."

A lengthy pause is followed by the crack of the hammer falling on the auctioneer's gavel. Sir Peter groans, "Not sold." The unwanted yearling is led out of the ring.

Six years later Sir Peter took just a few seconds to look at his notes before recalling, "There was no interest in him at all. At the time he was still small, a very late foal; he did not strike me very much then. Nobody was mad about Gala Performance in those days."

George Rogers had hovered at the side of the ring without bidding. He admits, "I just could not bring myself to nod for him. I stood and watched him being led out well below his reserve. I remember three or four good judges nearby agreeing he was simply not big enough despite his good pedigree."

33

Arthur Ryan's immediate dismay at the lack of interest swiftly turned to anger. Even in the late summer of 1979 the disbelief was still in his voice as he croaked, "There was not a single bid. Not one. The auctioneer made an awful mistake. Instead of looking for an opening bid of about the reserve or a bit less he doubled it and more. I felt that's that. It frightened everyone off. He looked for an opening bid of 3,500. Obviously everyone went on looking at their catalogues thinking it was absurd for him to be expecting 3,000 or so for that animal."

The next lot, a Bluerullah yearling owned by Arthur Ryan, was sold for 820 guineas. Bitterly upset, Arthur Ryan and his wife Elizabeth loaded Regina's rejected yearling into their small horse trailer and towed it back to Inch.

Peter Ryan, ringing from London that night, took the news philosophically. He recalls, "We knew the yearling would not fetch a high price so it was not such a bad blow. There was just a passing thought of keeping a yearling and having it in training. But we dismissed the idea and agreed to break him in and send him back to the sales."

A few weeks later Regina's unwanted yearling colt was turned down yet again, this time by John Murphy, who trains at the Curragh. While visiting studs in the district in search of potential material for his stable John was persuaded to call in at Inch. He recalls, "Mr Ryan wanted to sell the colt and I was prepared to look at him. We arrived on a cold winter's day to find this awfully small, really tiny little thing in a huge big box deep in straw. I would not bet on it that he stood even 14.3 hands high at the time." John Murphy remembers a price of £500 being mentioned. His friendly face creases into a huge grin as he laments, "I left him behind for no money at all. We were some judges that day."

The next spring Arthur Ryan began the delicate, time-consuming but satisfying task of breaking in the colt no one had wanted. He would spend half an hour or so each morning, lungeing him on a long rein, walking, trotting, cantering, first left handed and then right handed. Later he added side reins and a roller on his back where a saddle would eventually be placed. The colt, by now a 2-year-old, proved very easy to break. He had the right spirit. The time arrived for a human to perch across

34

his back. Arthur chose his second son Roland, slim and light. Monksfield accepted the unexpected burden with the good humour that has marked his career ever since. Arthur Ryan also persuaded a terrified farm boy to sit properly on the colt's back as he was led round the small yard.

Sale time was approaching, so to complete the young pupil's education in the final fortnight Arthur Ryan sent him the few miles to the Doyles' farm at Holy Cross. After two or three days Ryan was invited to see the 2-year-old ridden at speed for the first time. He found him being lunged round and round a manure heap on the edge of a large field.

"Their method", says Arthur drily, "was to keep him circling there until he was dripping with sweat and hardly able to lift his feet. Then the young girl held him while her brother climbed quietly into the saddle."

Away they charged across the field – by coincidence, the airfield where Arthur Ryan later learned to fly. The young rider, barely in control, and his steed disappeared out of sight over the brow of the hill. A few minutes later they came into view, happily still together, trotting back towards the group waiting apprehensively by the manure heap.

The 2-year-old, barely broken, was already entered in the late spring sales at Ballsbridge, traditionally held after the second day of Punchestown races in April. Arthur Ryan set off for Dublin, towing the trailer behind his car and was bemused to find the usually busy sales centre deserted. He waited for half an hour, then realized he had mistaken the date. Once more Monksfield returned to Inch.

On the correct day, May 17th 1974 Arthur Ryan was ill with flu. Defying a high temperature he drove to Dublin to discover that the sale ring had been moved a few hundred yards from its previous immaculate headquarters, sold to the Allied Irish Bank, to a small, cramped pen normally used for showing pigs. Goffs had tired of paying a rent based on turnover. They were planning to build their own modern complex at Kill much nearer the centre of Irish racing at the Curragh. Meanwhile they were forced to use the temporary accommodation offered at the show ground. Soon afterwards the Irish bloodstock sales industry split into two rival factions. Goffs moved into their showpiece centre

35

at Kill and a fresh company, Ballsbridge sales, emerged with new facilities and buildings on the site of the RDS showground. Thus the May 1974 sale was one of the last to be held by Goffs at Ballsbridge.

Arthur Ryan, unimpressed by such Irish intrigue, stumbled across to a nearby pub for a bowl of hot soup to ease his aching body. His wife Elizabeth stayed behind with the 2-year-old colt and, sure enough, saw the now familiar face of George Rogers coming to inspect Monksfield.

"I liked the family so much but each time I looked at him he seemed to be shrinking," George confesses. "I thought he was too small for one thing and he was a bad mover for another. No one else was interested that I could see."

"I intended to buy him, cut him straight away and turn him out in a field as a jumping store ... but he was not really big enough for that and he was a very late foal to run on the flat as a 2-year-old. I dithered for a while, but he was so small and oh ... *that action*," and his large hands show the curious winding action that has now become so famous.

Although George did not realize it at the time, someone else was interested in the much maligned 2-year-old whose breeding he coveted so much. A pale, dark haired young man, his left leg encased in plaster, hobbled awkwardly on crutches along to his box. After a long glance at the colt standing peacefully in the corner of his box, the young man and his wife moved on but returned shortly for a more prolonged appraisal. They watched eagerly as Monksfield was led out and walked up and down outside his box.

As the time for the sale drew near, Arthur Ryan, by now thoroughly miserable and unwell, had decided on a sensibly low reserve of 800 guineas. He did not intend to take the little colt home from Ballsbridge for a third time. As Elizabeth Ryan prepared to lead the 2-year-old colt into the ring, her husband, his temperature hovering close to 105°, made his way slowly towards the rostrum to find an absurdly young auctioneer feeling little better than himself.

Robert Hall, barely 20, the blond son of Goffs manager, was half-way through a nerve-racking half-hour session with the hammer on his very first day as a fully fledged auctioneer.

36

Robert's father, Captain Michael Hall, had joined Goffs in their infancy in 1949 when the annual turnover was averaging well below half a million pounds. When he retired in 1974 it had spiralled way over £5 million a year. In that time Captain Hall had sold many bargains including Hard Ridden, the Derby winner, for only 270 guineas and such future Grand National winners as L'Escargot, Mr What, Early Mist, Royal Tan, Anglo and Red Alligator. He had also knocked down Anzio, a future champion hurdler for a mere 500 guineas.

Now his son Robert was about to sell a bargain that would compare favourably with his father's triumphs. At school in Ireland Robert had been keen enough on racing at the age of 8 to buy the *Irish Field* rather than the *Eagle*. Since he'd left school he had worked first as a dogsbody for Goffs for £10 a week pocket money, completed a course at the National Stud, and visited the United States several times, taking a job on a stud, working for a sales company, and then putting in some time at an auctioneering college. There he was taught the finer (and tougher) American methods of selling such produce as tobacco and whisky in bulk. That contrasted enormously with his brief experience at home selling off, at the end of the day, horses that had failed to reach their reserves and were being re-offered to late comers and those who fancied a second attempt. "If I made a blunder it was not that serious," he concedes with a grin.

As Monksfield entered the hotch-potch sale ring in the white-washed pig shed, lined with stalls, Robert Hall, now elevated to a more important role, fidgeted with his hammer as he waited on the makeshift rostrum. He had been told of the previous failure to sell the colt but at least the breeder wheezing behind him had decided on a realistic reserve. The trusty Goffs' tapes take up the story in Robert Hall's anxious voice.

"What for the Gala Performance colt then? He's been broken in the last three weeks and has been lightly ridden and we've a vet's certificate that says he's sold sound. A thousand to start me please? Any bid of 1,000 to start me? 1,000, any bid of 1,000 please? 1,000, he'll make it and more," his voice does not sound convincing. "800 then, any bid of 800. Start me away please with 800, any bid of 800, six then, 600 to start me. Any bid of 600?"

It is an accepted practice for auctioneers to take bids from the wall or anywhere else until the reserve is reached. The idea is to break the ice and start the proceedings until the first genuine bid is made. Without a flicker of interest from the crowd packed tight against the tiny sales ring, Robert Hall invented a bid of 600 guineas.

"He was very small," Robert explains. "There was no interest in him. He was an extremely late foal and came into the ring immediately after three much older, more mature 2-year-olds." The young auctioneer had noted on his catalogue, "Small, 15½ hands? . . . attractive head, half-brother to three winners. Grandam Tambara."

On the tape Robert's voice, a shade more confidently, continues, "600. Thank you, sir. 600, 600, we'll go on at 600 now. At 600 for the Gala Performance. Half-brother to three winners," he throws in despairing of ever receiving a genuine bid. Then he noticed a slight flick of a catalogue by a man directly in front of him in the very first row of onlookers, leaning against the temporary rails, a pair of crutches under one arm.

Excitement enters his voice. "At 620 then, at 620, against my starter at 620, at 620, at 640 now, 640, 640, at 660 guineas, 660 guineas. At 680, 680, make it 700, at 680, have another, you've only had a couple you know, at 680 guineas. 700, thank you, 700 now, at 700 guineas. Are you bidding, sir? At 700, thank you, at 700, at 700 guineas. At 720 now, at 720, come again, at 720 guineas, you've only had the one, at 720 guineas, at 720, have another in front, at 720, you lose him at 720," his voice tails off in disappointment.

The man on crutches, staring intently, waved his catalogue again at 740 guineas and began to hope the colt might soon be on the market. Robert Hall, less certain, tried to tease another bid from the bored audience without response. Urgently he tapped his assistant on the arm to see if the breeder, lurking behind, would let the colt go at 740 guineas, fully 60 guineas below his reserve price. Arthur Ryan, tired, depressed, feeling desperately ill, nodded in resignation. Somewhere in the distance he heard the hammer drop at 740 guineas. Robert Hall swiftly sent an aide to find out the name of the buyer, the man leaning heavily on crutches, with a delighted smile spreading across his boyish face.

Hall recalls, "You are always disappointed when you fail to

make the reserve but if you can sell the horse at all then that is probably the market value at the time." Who was the underbidder? No one there that day seems to know. Possibly he was just an interested spectator trying to help the bidding along towards the reserve. Or maybe there was not a genuine bid at 720 guineas. Robert Hall cannot remember. George Rogers knows he should have tried to buy the colt instead of watching intently from his position at the ringside.

"I might have chanced one bid, but I don't think so," his voice falters at the thought of his plan to geld the 2-year-old.

The secret of the underbidder's identity may never be solved but Robert Hall did not have to wait long to find out who had made the final nod. Scribbled on his aide's form was the name of Des McDonogh.

# 4

# A woman is not
# a person

Totally dejected, Arthur Ryan exchanged a few pleasantries
with McDonogh and his wife Helen, before departing for Inch.
Monksfield spent the night at Ballsbridge for the good reason that
his new owner could not find a horse-box going in the direction
of his stables tucked away in the north corner of County Meath,
right on the border with County Cavan. Des McDonogh had
not really expected to buy anything that day.

He and Helen returned the following morning with a trailer
and Helen led Monksfield out of his box. Hobbling along behind
as best he could Des saw the colt start to jig-jog. "I had the fright
of my life. I thought, My God, he did not do *that* yesterday. He's
not right. He was winding his front legs, throwing them out
wide. Helen, in front, could not see and told me not to be
ridiculous. Once I looked at his head and deep girth again I was
happier. But that jig-jogging frightened me to death."

Des McDonogh had been training a handful of nonentities for
barely 18 months at Billywood Stud, a wet, confined cattle farm
near the village of Mullagh. So the beautifully bred colt came to
his new home whose complement at the time comprised a
couple of 3-mile chasers, a hunter chaser, one broken-down
hurdler, two very slow maidens on the flat and a few bullocks.
The only 2-year-old on the place, Monksfield was installed in a
cramped, ramshackle box that would not have looked out of
place in a knacker's yard.

Des McDonogh's rise to become the first Irish trainer since
Vincent O'Brien in the early 1950s to win two successive
Champion Hurdles with the same horse is one of the most

40

unlikely stories to emerge even from that land of fables.

Born on April 11th 1946, and raised in the suburbs of Limerick, he is the son of Clement McDonogh, a clerk for Esso at Shannon airport 16 miles away. His mother Margaret's eldest brother Frank Mulvihill, a marathon runner, was captain of the Irish athletic team in the 1948 London Olympics. His grandfather had a livery yard and undertaking business in the middle of bustling Limerick city and, with a nephew Joe, used to run the Limerick Harriers. Another uncle, Alf, spent much of his time buying horses to be sent to England for the British cavalry.

Des McDonogh's precocious talents at school were more artistic. Clear voiced and bright eyed he was the best singer in the choir and later became a gifted actor. Today he has added mimicry to his repertoire. Given the slightest encouragement he will slip into any number of amusing, recognizable accents. As a soprano at the tender age of 8, he was so small that when he sang in concert, even at full stretch, he could not reach the microphone at its lowest position, so a specially designed dias $2\frac{1}{2}$ feet high, painted silver, was built for him. His cherubic features and piping voice made him a natural for the parts of girls in several school operettas. Des relished singing in public, then and now, and has often said how much he would have liked to have been a professional actor or singer.

"Embarrassed? Not at all. If I was asked in the morning to sing in front of the Queen I'd be thrilled."

Away from school he yearned to ride ponies. He'd learned to ride, after a fashion, as a lad while on holiday at a cousin's farm. An enormous, gentle, work horse, tied loosely behind a pony and trap, had to be taken to be shod in Limerick nine miles away. Wearing shorts and wellington boots, Des was loaded on board the giant horse and bounced all the way to Limerick. Half-way back to the farm he finally learned how to rise to the trot, a painful lesson, for his calves and knees were raw by the end of the journey. At school he became friends with John Walsh whose parents kept several ponies and by the age of 12 he was riding at shows and hunting, equally adept with a saddle or bareback. He would cycle the eight miles there and back or, risking other boys' barbed humour, would catch a bus for most of the journey feeling conspicuous in jodhpurs, then walk the final two miles.

One summer John Walsh was sent away for a fortnight to work for trainer John Oxx at the Curragh. Des showed interest in a similar move and was introduced by the Walshs to Gerald Hogan, training successfully some 14 miles from Limerick; from that point he would cycle there on every possible occasion to ride out in the mornings and work in the yard.

Des McDonogh's passion for racing was fired by regular visits with his father to Limerick racecourse, just half a mile from his home. "Daddy loved racing and he always gave me two bob to put on each race on the Tote. I'd have my bet, then clamber up to my regular perch on the stands fence at a point where the rails were covered in chicken wire strong enough to hold my weight. The jockeys fascinated me and I was a great fan of Pat and Tos Taaffe."

Back at school his voice had deepened to baritone and he switched to acting, taking lead roles. In 'Private Secretary' he was on stage for two hours and found the adrenalin flowing freely as the audience reacted to his antics. He confesses, "I never learned my lines as such. I just used to take the cue line from the other person. If he missed the cue line I was out. I would always improvise and ad-lib." Only once did he forget his lines. Instantly he dropped all available props. In the subsequent uproar he called for a prompt and was away again.

Des left school aged 18 to begin a summer job with a car hire firm at £6 a week. This allowed him time to ride out for Gerald Hogan at the weekends and continue his burgeoning career with the 67 Drama Group in the city. He admits, "I loved being on the stage, the centre of attention, always in comedy parts. I like to make people laugh." The only serious role he played was in 'Twelve Angry Men'. A favourite comedy was 'Charley's Aunt' which played to packed houses of 400 throughout its run.

Flattering reviews appeared in the local papers. One critic wrote, "This highly amusing play is a triumph for Des McDonogh who portrays Charley's Aunt so well." Another said, "Des McDonogh as Charley's Aunt is really first class. His facial expressions and gestures had one howling with laughter all through. He certainly has a talent for making people laugh. Once or twice it looked as if he had even broken the concentration of some of his fellow players with his tricks. For Des McDonogh's

# Charley's Aunt
## GOOD FUN, HEARTY LAUGHS

After an absence of seve... ars, the ageless *C...* *...nt* returned to Lim... is week to spend four nights ... Amharclann na Feile — ...ursday through Sunday. A ...oup of young boys and ...ls who call themselves the ...7 Club" hoping to reinterest ...ung Limerick people in ...eatre, are running it.

...t is entirely their own all-...ateur production — they ...n painted and designed ...ir own sets. Most of the ...yers are making their stage ...ut, but due to an admirable ...m spirit and near-slavery, ...y have overcome most of ... faults one might expect. ...uite honestly, it is the ...niest *Charlie's Aunt* I have ... seen and that is saying

something. Des McDonagh as *Charlie's Aunt* is really first class. His facial expressions and gestures had me howling with laughter all through. Des certainly has a great talent for making people laugh, once or twice it looked as if he had even broken the concentration of some of his fellow-players with his tricks. Brendan Lane and Paul Reeves give truly professional performances.

Martin Daly and Kathleen LeGear, fit their parts very well. Kieran Martin, Noel O'Connor, Biddy Keogh, Geraldine Costelloe and Eilis O'Connell all have their moments.

For Des McDonagh's performance alone this production is well worth going to see; that he is supported so well ensures your enjoyment. The curtain goes up at 8.15 p.m. and when it comes down I bet you have a large pain in your sides from laughing.

———I.M.

The cast of Charley's Aunt with Des McDonogh sitting (bottom left).
*Credit: Limerick Leader*

An admiring note from a critic in the local paper.

performance alone this production is well worth going to see.''

Other leading parts followed in 'The Country Boy', 'O'Flaherty V.C.' and he drew more admiring notices for his portrayal of Herr Winkelkopf in 'Lord Savile's Crime'. One impressed critic wrote "Herr Winkelkopft, an insane anarchist, is played by Des McDonogh. This character should provide comedy in the truest sense and his slapstick farce and cynicism should draw streams of laughter.''

Clearly he had the necessary talent, so why did he not become a professional actor? Des shrugs, "I only needed the slightest push at the time and I would have gone off to drama school. But I suppose the lure of racing was even stronger.''

Rugby took up his spare time. He played for his school and, though light and small, was a key regular for the Old Crescent team. "I always played better when I got a 'tump' early in the game. I'm only a little fellow and I needed to get my blood up and have a bit of temper to play at my best.'' Once, when he was playing for Old Crescent in the Munster Senior Cup, he was raked deliberately by a hefty opponent. The scrum collapsed, McDonogh was pinned underneath on his back and an opposing forward twice dragged a boot across his head. Luckily the ten stitches needed were under the hairline.

When the job with the cab firm folded Des worked full time for six months, unpaid, for Gerald Hogan. His whole aim was to achieve just one ride as an amateur jockey. An unambitious young man, then and now, his racing horizon reached only as far as Limerick races. One ride there in front of his father and he would be content. Once he walked all the way back to Limerick after a disagreement with the trainer. Finally on St Stephen's Day, 1965, Gerald Hogan fulfilled his promise and gave Des a ride on the unraced Fugleman in a novice hurdle at Limerick. The McDonogh household buzzed with anticipation that Christmas. After a typically solid and happy family Christmas lunch Des wandered along the half mile or so to the deserted grandstand, vaulted over the rails and earnestly walked every yard of the $1\frac{1}{2}$ mile hurdle course.

He recalls, "I was dying of nerves but was sure I'd win.'' Des and his father worked out an intricate system of signals before he walked out, legs shaking, to the parade ring. If Gerald Hogan thought Fugleman would win Des would hold his whip in his left hand. If Fugleman was not expected to do well, he would keep the stick in his right hand. His father, watching intently on the edge of the paddock, saw Des clutching his whip in his left hand. Swiftly he moved into battle in the betting ring and so missed the sight of Des cantering gingerly to the starting gate with the whip in his right hand. His face crinkles with laughter as he recalls, "Daddy thought our boy Des was going to do it and away he went and backed me at 33/1 and we finished last. Fugleman jumped well enough but he was terribly slow and proved useless afterwards."

After six months with Gerald Hogan Des felt it was time to start earning his living. His father found him a job as a clerk for a small airline based at Shannon; Des was due to become a dispatch officer but the airline folded nine months later. Next he tried his skills as a salesman for a meat company, driving around the country delivering to shops. "It was a miserable job. I never thought anything could be so difficult in all my life. We had to finish the route each day and I'd take 17 or sometimes 18 hours." He was keen to go on a rugby tour with the Crescent club to St Ives. The meat company did not like the idea of his taking a holiday then. After consultation with his understanding father Des left anyway for a memorable tour of Cornwall; then returned to start a fresh job as a dispatch clerk in the Limerick offices of Irish Wire Products. It seemed a bit of a dead end. He says, "I was shoved from one department to have a bit more responsibility in another, in charge of organization, wages and bonus schemes." Still at weekends he would cycle, or drive out to Gerald Hogan's stable.

The odd moderate ride came his way in races and Gerald had begun to put him up in point-to-points. One day the mercurial Barry Brogan, whose career later turned disastrously wrong, was brought in to ride four horses for Hogan. The first three ran so badly that Des McDonogh replaced Barry on the last one, which finished second. Des was totally dependent on Gerald Hogan for any chance mounts but his firm did not like his taking holidays in odd days and afternoons to ride in races. Eventually he was summoned before the company secretary, who demanded pompously, "Which is more important your job or

45

No. She did not fall. Helen McDonogh's marvellous balance helped Hilbre recover from this dreadful blunder.
*Credit: Irish Times*

your riding?" Des counted very slowly to ten then fled from the room muttering furiously.

At last he was given a good point-to-point ride by Gerald Hogan on an old handicapper, Gambler's Choice, in a novice riders' event at the Ward Union Hunt. Des was able to lie second for most of the way, led jumping the last fence and just held off the furious late challenge of Felspar, ridden by a younger, unknown rival. To his dismay the judge, standing on bales of straw by the winning post, called a dead heat.

"I knew I'd won. I was in front all the way to the line and could see his head just behind mine but I was happy enough with a dead heat. I'd still won. The old horse did it all. I was really a passenger."

His young rival that day, aged 16, was none other than the redoubtable Ted Walsh, champion Irish amateur many times since and winner of some 400 races. Ted confirms, "Des won by a head and I was relieved when a dead heat was called. I think the judge knew we were both beginners and felt it would be fairest to share the prize."

Celebrations that night were suitably wild but throughout the evening Des and his father sipped only soft drinks. McDonogh was teetotal and his son has followed suit. He took a vow of total abstinence at his Confirmation and has never broken it. At Pony Club he once downed twenty-four glasses of Coca Cola. "I was always able to enjoy myself and entertain people without drinking."

Des and his girlfriend were invited in Dorothy Hogan's party to a Hunt Ball. Also in the group was Helen Bryce-Smith, the leading girl rider in Ireland. Helen had run up a string of point-to-point victories on several horses including an astonishing thirty-four on Still William and twenty-six on Star News. Helen was a tough, highly competent jockey and the fact sometimes annoyed her usually placid brother John. In the Ward Union

But they did fall at the same fence on the next circuit!
*Credit: Irish Times*

Open race she rode the trusty Still William against John on the ex-chaser Irish Coffee. With a circuit to go the race lay between them. John was just in front after jumping the next fence and was not at all pleased to see his sister creeping boldly up his inside before a sharp right hand bend. He moved over to stop her coming through. She pushed back to prevent Still William running out. John remembers, "We were locked together, neither would give way, and in the end her horse fell and brought mine down." Both horses and jockeys were all right but the sound of the swearing match between brother and sister could be heard three fields away.

Helen, then, was the girl Des monopolized at the Hunt Ball that night. "Funnily enough I was mad about the girl I took to the Ball yet I spent the entire evening talking to Helen. I'd had a bad fall on my head that day so I expect I was talking nonsense."

They started going out together and sometimes Des would stay the occasional weekend with her parents who trained with great success at Cherrymount House, Moynalty, in County Meath. Des timed his summer holiday to be there, riding and helping in the yard. At the end of the fortnight the Bryce-Smiths gave him a ride in an amateurs' race at Kilbeggan.

Matters progressed. The Bryce-Smiths' head man was retiring. If there was a position going Des was interested. After consulting his parents, who always gave him maximum support, Des handed in his notice at the Irish Wire Company and started a new phase in his life. He explains, "At Limerick I was beginning to be a zombie . . . just going three hundred yards to work in the morning and coming back home in the evening. I did not see that I was getting anywhere and could not face the thought of forty more years there before I got a little presentation on retirement. Here was a chance to learn more in a stable, with a good record, where things were done well. At once I seemed to be riding better horses in work and to be going faster on them. It was then that training horses for a living came into my mind for the first time."

Helen's parents had bought Cherrymount, a farm with some 200 acres, extremely cheaply at the end of the Second World War. Her mother Jean was a gifted rider and spent many years as assistant to her father G. P. Sanday, who was a leading trainer in

48

the 1920s. Sitting in the McDonoghs' kitchen with her two granddaughters squeaking at her feet the formidable Mrs Jean Bryce-Smith recalls, "My father was one hell of a gambler. He would look at the form book and by the time we reached the races we were certain to win and £500 would go on. As a child I would often start at one end of the bookies with fivers and he would work his way along from the other end until we met in the middle."

Hairpin, bought for £35, won over thirty races for him and landed one of his biggest gambles in the Grand Annual Chase at Cheltenham. Sanday took Jean along to Chester to help choose a present for her mother, a brooch that cost £1,000.

"Which year was that?" I inquired innocently.

"1923 wasn't it?" she replied as if I had asked a daft question.

Tall, grey haired, with pale blue eyes, Mrs Jean Bryce-Smith is a forceful personality and an amusing raconteur but when she makes a statement she looks firmly at you as if to defy any contradiction. She was a fearless rider in point-to-points but earned severe disapproval in Cheshire society when she had the nerve to race against men rivals and, even worse, beat them. "They created hell. Everyone went for my mother and she never let me ride against men again. People frowned on girls riding in races against men in those days you know."

Even the bold Jean Sanday, just 14, met her match the day she faced the Stewards at Haydock Park. She had been standing by the last fence when her father's horse fell while challenging for the lead. The jockey was injured, no other runners appeared, so Jean vaulted neatly into the saddle and cantered past the post, knowing the rule at the time stated that any person could weigh-in if a horse was remounted after the last fence. Encouraged by that marvellous pair of jockeys Billy Stott and Billy Speck she marched into the weighing room and sat on the scales.

"The only thing is," called Speck, "can you do the weight?"

"I can do it and more," she replied forcibly, explaining for my benefit, "It did not matter if you were overweight."

According to the rules the horse was entitled to second place money but I fear news of the women's liberation movement had not quite reached the ears of the crusty Haydock Stewards almost 50 years ago.

Jean Bryce-Smith snorts at the memory. "They disqualified me from having second money because they ruled a woman was not a person. What *cheek*. Me not a person! There was the most fearful row, don't you know." A triumphant gleam enters her eye. "They changed the rule after that."

Many years later, in December 1968, her daughter Helen was involved in a similar furore with the Irish Turf authorities. Helen and Jean Moore, a brilliant girl rider, had shaken the complacency of Irish racing by applying for licences to ride against men. Helen explains, "Our application was confined to amateur races so nobody could accuse us of trying to do the professionals out of their livelihood. We had both ridden lots of point-to-point winners. All we wanted to do was take on the men in bumper races. We did not need anyone to fuss over us. My friend Jean would cut your nose off to win a race. Me? I'd not give anyone an inch." Her brother John no doubt agrees with that.

Their bid for emancipation on Ireland's racecourses met initial resistance and then an unequivocal refusal. The Irish Turf Club announced haughtily, "The Stewards are of the opinion that race riding in open competition can be a dangerous business for professionals and a dangerous and hazardous sport for the amateur. To grant permission to ladies would not be in the best interests of racing."

Lord Holmpatrick, with quaint old-fashioned ideals, commented for the Turf Club, "The decision has more than a little element of gallantry in it. How would a male jockey react if he found a woman jockey coming up the inside of the track? Would he be likely to gallop over a rider in trouble if he knew she was a woman?"

Despite this setback girl riders eventually achieved a major breakthrough, particularly in Ireland where Joanna Morgan, an attractive wisp of a girl from the Welsh valleys, broke new ground as a successful flat race apprentice. She's now a competent lightweight rider and was considered good enough by trainer Seamus McGrath to partner his horse Riot Helmet in the 1976 Irish Sweeps Derby at the Curragh.

When Jean Sanday met her future husband Cyril Bryce-Smith, a soft spoken, gentle man, at a party in London, he was working in a wine shop and had no interest in racing at all. She

A youthful Paddy Broderick (right) riding out for Cyril
Bryce-Smith.    *By courtesy of the Irish Press Ltd, Dublin*

laughs, "I soon changed that." They moved to Ireland and
swiftly established one of the most successful stables in the
country.

Jean Bryce-Smith taught her two children to ride by the
simplest of methods. Perched on a bicycle herself, with a child's
seat behind the saddle, she would lead a small pony. John and
Helen would take turns on the pony; but as soon as she could ride
well Helen found show jumping very boring because, she says, it
was too slow.

Helen was riding work regularly on racehorses by the age of
12. Several well-known jockeys also began their racing careers at
Cherrymount, including Cathal Finnegan, John Burke, Gabriel
Curran and Night Nurse's popular battered partner Paddy
Broderick.

Says Jean, "Paddy had the most wonderful hands and he never
complained. After the most terrible falls he would not say a
word. His favourite entertainment was pitch and toss in Moynalty village. At the time he was earning a few shillings a week

A winning team. Helen McDonogh and the faithful Still William. Together they won 34 point-to-points.

*Photo: Irish Field*

he once came home with £100 in his pocket." Tommy Kinane, too, rode occasionally for the stable. "Tommy was utterly fearless, a bit dashing as a jockey. He always went straight to the front whatever you told him to do. He was a character, a rough and tumble jockey, you know; as hard as he could go, as fast as he could go for as long as he could go." Sometimes Paddy led round a horse at the races ridden by Tommy.

When she was 12 Helen was given Boltown Comet by her parent's neighbour Captain Gerald Maguire. Boltown Comet had been unmanageable at the Curragh, failed to reach his reserve at the sales and in his early days at Cherrymount devoured the stable's pet hen who roosted on the rafters of his box. Quickly gelded, he proved a high-class hurdler but after he won the Coronation Hurdle at Liverpool the stuffy English

Jockey Club did not like the idea of a minor owning a racehorse.

Jean roars, "They hummed and they hawed and in the end they let us keep the prize but insisted we changed the ownership." Boltown Comet continued to win, in Jean's name, until Vincent O'Brien rang one day, called at the yard and bought him a few weeks before the 1956 Champion Hurdle at Cheltenham. There he started second favourite to improve Vincent's astounding record in the race, but he failed to show his best form for his new trainer and finished only ninth of fourteen to Doorknocker.

Still William finished second in his two hurdle races before Jean Bryce-Smith gave him to Helen to ride in point-to-points. A small, typically chunky Vulgan gelding, he often carried 4 stone or more of lead in the saddle to compensate for Helen's featherweight. He won the majority of his races, always going the shortest way round, but sometimes would fall after a minor mistake, perhaps because the huge amount of dead weight on his withers made it difficult for him to regain his balance.

Still William's marvellous run of victories ended tragically in 1967, when he put his foot in a hidden drain during a race and broke his back. His body was brought back to Cherrymount and buried in a quiet, shaded corner of the Bryce-Smiths' favourite work ground, not far from two sets of schooling fences. A headstone, by his grave, proclaims simply, "Still William, winner of 34 point-to-points ridden by his owner."

# 5

# 'That Fabulous Head'

Des spent four years at Cherrymount, learning all the time. Often he would lead up Helen's mounts in point-to-points. "She was a brilliant rider and understood racing a lot more than I did. At that stage I did not know what it was like to ride a good horse and I still don't in a race." His career as an amateur rider was finished by a bone-crushing fall almost before it had begun, but he is the first to admit he was not exactly ideal jockey material. "At home it's different. There's no man better to ride a bit of work than me. You show horses gentleness and kindness, you know what they can do and you never persuade them to reveal what's there. Whereas in a race all the jockeys are looking for it and you have to look for it too. I just don't have the knack to do that."

He finished fourth on the Bryce-Smiths' Nicky's Vulgan at Naas and was not surprised to be called before the Stewards. "I panicked, pulled out my stick and went at it, head down, as hard as I could. I swung at her twenty times and maybe touched her twice. When I got off no one said a word." The Stewards' film showed McDonogh whirling his whip like a windmill on a windy day and Nicky's Vulgan corkscrewing from one side of the track to the other and back again, taking horses with her. A stern lecture followed before he left the room a thoroughly deflated young man. Inevitably when the mare won next time he was not riding her.

Three weeks later he was given another chance by the Bryce-Smiths at Downpatrick on Pitroddie in an amateur riders handicap hurdle. He was changing in the corner of the weighing room when he was joined by Frank Carroll, a kind man and a wily jockey. Frank told him, "Only one professional in ten can use a whip properly. One in ten. The horse will do as much for you if you slap him down the shoulder and just keep him balanced, rather than waving your stick all over the place. When it's time to ask the question just give him a couple of slaps and push with hands and heels." Refreshed by such sensible advice Des rode Pitroddie with new confidence, challenged between two rivals after jumping the final hurdle and forged clear to win by a length. It was his first win apart from point-to-points.

Helen and her mother shared the training. Des studied their methods and has followed them. He does not overwork his horses at home, does not gallop them flat-out and schools them carefully until they are good jumpers.

The romance between Des and Helen blossomed. They took a rare weekend off to travel over to watch the 1970 Grand National. On the boat bound for Holyhead they ate breakfast next to a table where a man ordered two boiled eggs, one brown and one white; the brown egg to be boiled for 3 minutes and the white egg for $3\frac{1}{2}$ minutes. The trip was also memorable for the way a young jockey, Brian Fletcher, took the time to show them some of the more daunting fences on the course and for a very easy win in the Grand National by Gay Trip, one of only seven finishers.

The young couple wanted a home of their own and, despite some parental disapproval at Cherrymount, they married in October 1971, and moved into a tiny, damp cottage on the edge of Mullagh lake, after a brief honeymoon in England when Des was forced to retire to bed for a week with a severe attack of sinus. On their return they resumed working for Helen's parents until they could move two miles away into a small, run-down, 70-acre dairy farm, Billywood Stud, bought for Helen as a wedding present. Overrun with weeds and high grass, with just a cow byre, grain loft and a lean-to shed to accompany the cramped bungalow, it was the most unlikely setting for an equine fairytale. But Des and Helen were determined to make the break, to train a few hunters and point-to-pointers and farm the land as best they could.

Their plans suffered a cruel setback in March 1972, when a

Des McDonogh returns on his last winner All Bloom, at Down Royal, led in by Joe Brady, and followed by Helen.
*Credit: Irish Field.*

comparatively simple fall broke Des' left shin in three places and some bones in his foot as the horse rolled over on impact. For the first few weeks he was immobile and moped miserably at the cottage while Helen continued to work for her parents. Later, as soon as he was able to walk on crutches, she would drop him off at their new home where a clutch of poplar trees stood sentry at the entrance to the short drive. There, painfully and laboriously, with one leg encased in plaster, sometimes resting on a cushion, sometimes on an oil drum, he converted the lean-to shed into the absurdly small box that now houses Monksfield.

Perched on the cushion, armed with a coal shovel, he dug out the foundations of the shed to make it deep enough to accommodate three boxes. Tony Grady, a friend from Cherrymount, would come down after evening stables to help put in the floors of the three boxes. Monksfield's box, just a few paces from the bungalow's back door and the two adjoining it, were built from spare bits and pieces of material. The doors had been thrown out by a nearby stud. Monksfield's earthenware manger, cracked and broken in several places when scrapped at Cherrymount, was patiently pieced together. When he found a small space on the wall that he could not fill, Des put in an old window taken from the bungalow. He added a similar window at the rear when he ran out of timber.

He explains, "The blocks were going so crooked and so high that if I'd put any more on the whole thing would have fallen down. So I finished it with timber." A large pillar remains at one end of the box with a narrow gap beside it. The roof does not have any felt under it. Only when Monksfield won his first Champion Hurdle was the box plastered on the inside. A diesel tank hangs on the outside wall. Behind is the tack room. Des McDonogh's attempt to tidy the front of the box by laying down a concrete passage was destroyed by the first heavy lorry to rumble over the thinly laid cement.

Smart surroundings don't make horses run any faster and you can understand Des McDonogh insisting, "I know it's the worst box in the yard but I would not swop it for £1,000. It's a landmark and I don't think I could ever knock it down."

The McDonoghs finally moved into Billywood in the summer of 1972 as soon as the bungalow was habitable. A

57

month later the plaster was removed from his left leg, but he was in such pain that he eventually moved back into hospital for a further manipulative operation that brought only temporary relief.

In November 1972 he took out a licence to train, to run a 3-year-old hurdler, Bright Record, housed in the old milking parlour. Initially his fees were just £1 a day but they rose 100 per cent to £2 a day 18 months later. The stable's gallops were, by conventional standards, non-existent. Des was and to some degree still is confined to cantering his horses round and round small, tight fields on the farm. He did build a 2½ furlong straight, uphill, all-weather gallop diagonally across the largest field but months of hard work were lost when the gallops were swept away by the first heavy rain of the winter. Later, with the help of neighbours, especially Farrell O'Reilly, he pushed out some hedges to give him more galloping space. In Ireland, at the time, if you wanted to train racehorses you simply applied for, and received, a licence from the Irish Turf Club. It's not so simple in Britain where the Jockey Club, in their wisdom, send round stable inspectors before granting a licence. Normally they choose retired policemen, whose knowledge of such matters is strictly limited, but even they would have wondered at Des McDonogh's lack of facilities. In Britain, certainly, he would not have been given a licence to train.

His first winner, in February 1973, was Maraka, a mare who had broken down and had been trained previously both by Helen's father and her brother John. Helen, particularly, spent hours on Maraka giving her plenty of regular, light exercise to strengthen her leg. Maraka finished fourth on her first outing, then won by a short head at Naas on February 1st.

Cyril Bryce-Smith, who had been ill for some time, lived just long enough to applaud his son-in-law's first win as a trainer. He died on February 25th 1973, and his wish to be buried alongside Still William was carried out. A bishop consecrated the ground at the funeral, his grave was railed off, and Cyril Bryce-Smith was buried with his racing silks in the peaceful corner of the schooling ground.

Two more wins followed that first hesitant year. Helen's point-to-pointer Blue Towser won a hunter chase at Ballinrobe

58

and best of all, Mrs Hawkins, slow and desperately lacking in ability, walked over for a prize of £297 in a maiden at Sligo.

Early in 1974 Des McDonogh's leg was so painful that he was forced into hospital for yet another operation. This time the surgeon spotted the reason for his constant discomfort. He found further damage to the foot that had not been highlighted by previous X-rays and decided a bone graft was the one certain way to cure the injury. The surgeon took a piece of shin bone, eight inches long, and knitted it to the damaged foot. In hospital for a further three weeks, Des watched Cheltenham races on television and was impressed by Lanzarote's victory in the Champion Hurdle.

"I loved the scenes at Cheltenham", he recalls, "but I could not believe we would ever possibly be part of them. We were terribly unambitious people. I could not see myself being involved with horses in a big way. We just hoped to be self-sufficient and keep the odd horse around the place. Helen would not have been happy away from horses and neither would I."

Bored, inactive and not a little depressed on his return to Billywood, his left leg still in plaster, Des decided to go to the Ballsbridge sales on May 17th without an idea of what was likely to pass through the ring. "We certainly were not well enough known to have a catalogue sent to us in advance by Goffs." As soon as Helen finished riding out they set off on the hour's run to Dublin and bought a catalogue at the entrance to the sale. Des McDonogh is not an envious man but he remembers looking through the names in that mixed sale knowing he could not possibly afford the pick of the list.

Together they began to wander round the clutch of boxes, checking individuals against their names in the catalogue, until they came upon Elizabeth Ryan sitting quietly outside the box containing Regina's freshly broken 2-year-old. Des recalls, "I opened the door and *that* was it, the way he looked at me from the corner of his box. He perked up as if to say, 'What the hell do you want?' I loved that head, that *fabulous* head, the instant I saw it. Helen liked him just as much, and his pedigree was good, but we bought him on the way we first set eyes on him in the box – though we later had him out and walked, but not trotted, up and down. I noticed he was a little long of his pasterns but really I

59

could not take my eyes off his beautiful head."

They inspected a few more possibles with waning interest then came back to Monksfield. Says Des, "It all depended on the money. He had good conformation, a nice depth, even though he was small. But I did not have any prospective owners and could not afford more than £700."

Elizabeth Ryan confirmed the colt was quiet, had been driven and backed, but the McDonoghs dared not be too excited. Funds were short and if the bidding started as low as 1,000 guineas they knew they were lost. Des agrees, "I was *mad* to have him but thought I had no chance really." Even so he raised his limit to £800 and was not going to bid for anything else until the colt had been through the ring. They made for the makeshift sale arena with a friend, Jack Hogan, who was interested in the lot before Monksfield, a large horse that was led out unsold and bought by Jack immediately afterwards outside the ring.

Monksfield stepped into the small circle and Des McDonogh was almost certainly the first to make a genuine bid. "I think young Hall ran him for a bit. I can't remember who was against me. The place was black with people and I could only see Monksfield's head above the mass crowded all round."

Des McDonogh first bid at 620 guineas, again at 660 and thought, for one heady moment during a brief lull he had him at 700 guineas. As the bidding jumped to 720 guineas he came back quickly at 740 guineas with another wave of his catalogue. "Even then I did not think I'd get him because I was sure he was not yet on the market. There was a hurried conversation behind the rostrum and the next thing he was mine. We did not know the auctioneer and he certainly did not know us but his man had no difficulty finding me because I had gone beetroot colour and was quite delighted with myself."

Jack Hogan, bustling back into the ring after sealing his own deal, could not believe Des McDonogh had bought such a small colt. "Surely not that little thing," he chided, "come and see the lovely big horse I've bought." Poor Jack. His bargain never ran and eventually ended up at the kennels.

# 6

## 'I thought he was sure to win the Derby'

At the time they bought Monksfield the McDonoghs did not employ anyone to work for them, so while Des was in plaster Helen simply rode all the horses out herself. If they were away racing their neighbour Felix McCabe would pop round to feed the horses and check that everything was in order. A delightful man with a bright, impish face permanently topped by a cap in or out of the house, Felix is a bachelor farmer who met Des and Helen on his fishing trips to Mullagh lake. The trusty Felix McCabe was keeping an eye on things at Billywood when Monksfield arrived the day following the sale. Felix has since become Monksfield's chief source of his favourite Granny Smith apples but their relationship might have been put on a sounder, more lucrative footing the first time they met.

Helen unloaded Monksfield and led him round the yard while Des asked Felix his opinion. "Des wanted me to take a half share with him there and then", recalls Felix in his soft, peaty tones, "but I was not keen. Not at all. I did not like to say anything about the way the colt was walking and when he trotted, well, he *threw* his front legs out in a big circle."

Des McDonogh could not afford to keep the colt for long so he began looking for possible buyers. The first man he tried, an existing owner in the yard, lived in County Dublin and Des put the matter to him that very night over supper. Unaware of the rare jewel slipping at that moment through his fingers, he declined the offer and shortly afterwards moved his other horse away from the stable.

Undeterred, Des tried another established owner but he

61

preferred to wait for something better! He, too, moved his horse away later, now trains for himself and has been seen to shake his head with a certain studied disbelief at Monksfield's achievements.

For the first month or so Helen cantered the stable's new 2-year-old on his own round a harrowed circle of plough of perhaps 2½ furlongs. He seemed a bright, intelligent individual, good natured, a horse that did not need to be taught anything twice and so was at once nicknamed Smarty. But he was backward, a very late foal, and to their immense credit his new handlers had the good sense to give him the quietest possible introduction to their unconventional training methods.

The stable had not had a winner for exactly a year, since Mrs Hawkins' walk-over, when Des and Helen set off for Roscommon races on June 10th with Kavala, an honest but ordinary handicap chaser they trained for Mrs Jean Bryce-Smith. Kavala had finished fourth once from five runs for them in the preceding months but thrived on the prevailing hard ground and was as fit as he would ever be. Just before the race Des ran into his uncle Paddy Mulvihill, who introduced him to an old friend, Dr Michael Mangan, back on holiday in his native Ireland from his job as a radiologist at a hospital in St John's, Newfoundland. Paddy Mulvihill realized Des was in a hurry to saddle Kavala and asked where they might meet later. With uncharacteristic bravado Des pointed firmly to the winner's enclosure and called out, "There, after you've backed Kavala." Paddy Mulvihill and Michael Mangan hustled off to the betting ring, backed Kavala at 12/1 and watched with mounting excitement as he ran home first 1½ lengths in front of the odds-on favourite.

I doubt if a happier group has ever assembled in the winner's enclosure at Roscommon. Des had finally broken his long, lean spell, his mother-in-law was thrilled at her horse winning and Paddy Mulvihill with all his friends had backed the horse at extremely lucrative odds, though Michael Mangan reveals, "I gave Paddy £10 to back the horse but he shook his head as if I was a bloody fool and only put £2 on." The party soon adjourned to the nearest racecourse bar where Dr Mangan, impressed by the young trainer's approach, mentioned that for years his ambition had been to own a horse in training. Had Des McDonogh anything for sale? It seemed an ideal opportunity for Des to pass on Smarty; certainly he had nothing else for sale and Michael Mangan's interest was aroused when he was told the colt's breeding.

He explains, "Des and Helen's mother outlined the implications of owning a racehorse and mentioned the breeding of Smarty. I had followed the breeding of American horses sufficiently to know the impressive racing record of Native Dancer, Gala Performance's sire. When they added that the colt was out of a Tulyar mare I became fantastically interested and arranged to go and see him at their stables as soon as possible."

Who better to accompany Michael Mangan and his wife Sheila than their old friend Father Paddy McDermott, curate of Balcarra, County Mayo, a man with extensive knowledge of horses stretching back to the time two generations of his family had purchased horses for the British army. Father McDermott's hobby was and is, to buy young horses, sometimes at Ballinasloe fair, break them in and educate them before selling them on.

The visit to see Smarty was a complete success. Michael Mangan recalls, "We spent the whole day at Billywood and I thought the colt was smashing, he had something about him. He was small all right but at the time I did not know how big a 2-year-old should be. I did not have a clue," he confesses with engaging candour, adding, "When I bought him I thought he was sure to win the Derby. I was very interested and would probably have bought him whatever Father Paddy thought." Before a deal was struck, before even he knew the price, Father Paddy McDermott, to his great credit, told Michael Mangan, "I'd give anything for that horse. *Anything.*"

Enchanted by the bright little colt, intrigued by the young trainer and his hard-working wife, Dr Mangan recalls, "I was completely overwhelmed by the idea of buying this horse who so obviously would be looked after with love and affection by this devoted couple." He agreed to pay £1,125, wrote out the cheque on the spot and called the colt Monksfield after the guesthouse which his mother had run for so many happy years of his childhood in the Salthill district of Galway.

Des McDonogh had already explained the horse would not be ready to run until the very end of the flat season. Michael

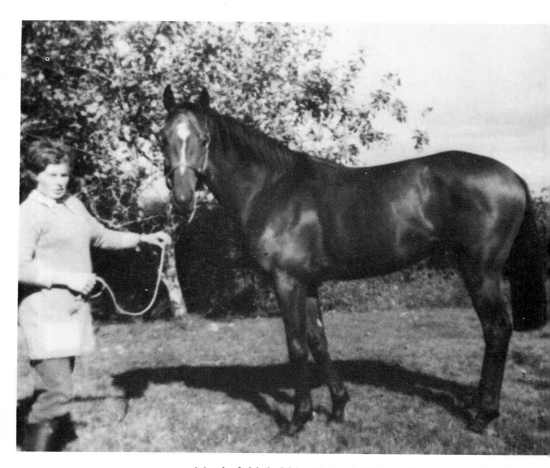

Monksfield, held by Helen McDonogh, poses on the day
he was bought by Michael Managan as a 2-year-old.

Mangan accepted the situation and at no stage in their long
partnership together has ever tried to interfere with the pattern
of races his trainer has mapped out for Monksfield. Dr Mangan
returned to Newfoundland while his new purchase, the first
racehorse he had owned, continued his light routine on the
plough. Eventually, when the autumn rain softened the ground,
Des took him to a neighbour's field where he was able to work 6,
almost 7 furlongs at a nice pace; then Monksfield, always ridden
by Helen, started to work upsides with Kavala.

Des, watching as his leg healed slowly, realized at once that
Monksfield was not a sprinter, but he did seem to build up an
impressive crescendo at the end of a gallop, his front legs going
in all directions. The trainer's initial panic at the strange sight had

mellowed to faint concern, for although the action looked appalling Helen assured him that, from the saddle, the colt seemed to move freely with a good stride.

It was time to enter Monksfield for one educational run on the flat at the end of the season. Des chose a 7½ furlong race at Punchestown which had the added advantage of an old-style start without stalls. He also entered Ettridge, a promising chaser who had won a novice event in September. Des wrote to Dr Mangan telling him of the plan to run Monksfield in a maiden plate on October 23rd and booked 29-year-old Ken Coogan for the ride. First jockey to Sir David Ainsworth, Ken was a cheerful little man with a reputation for looking after young horses. He had ridden only a handful of winners that season and was already thinking of trying his luck abroad.

Des McDonogh hoped Monksfield might finish in the middle of the field, running on, but this did not deter Dr Mangan from asking his mother-in-law to put £10 on for him on the Tote. Early on the morning of October 23rd Monksfield and Ettridge set off for Punchestown races, driven by Des McDonogh in an old converted bright red cattle lorry he had bought from his uncle's garage in Limerick for £1,200.

Paddy Mulvihill had arranged to meet him at the races but failed to show up. Monksfield was impressively calm and relaxed as Helen led him round the parade ring but Ken Coogan feared he was in for yet another bad ride of the kind that were increasingly being offered to him. Matisse, trained by the old master Paddy Prendergast, was a hot favourite in the race while Monksfield was one of only three debutantes in the field of fourteen.

As Ken Coogan padded into the paddock with the other jockeys he glanced at Monksfield and noted that he looked well but was possibly too fat to do himself full justice. He listened intently as Des told him to ensure he jumped off with the others. Says Des, "I was a bit worried he might be left at the tapes start, which he had not seen before, and emphasized the horse was so lazy that Ken would probably have to wake him up to stay in touch." Des left the paddock, told some friends from Limerick not to back Monksfield, then joined Helen on the stands to watch the runners canter down to the start. Matisse was by then

Monksfield wins on his racecourse debut at the
astounding Tote odds of 647–1, ridden by Ken Coogan.
*Credit: Irish Independent*

a 5/4 favourite with Monksfield priced at 25/1 with several other
forlorn hopes.

Ken Coogan remembers, "Even though there was a nice bit of
cut in the ground I was not very impressed with Monksfield on
the way to the start. When the race began he was close to the back
but after we had gone a furlong I gave him a root in the belly and
to my surprise he started to pass horse after horse."

Closing relentlessly on the leaders Monksfield moved
smoothly into third place entering the straight, eased through
into second and then, to the amazement of just about everyone at
Punchestown, quickened to catch and pass Matisse in the final
furlong with Ken Coogan sitting as quietly on his back as a
church mouse. Christy Roche, who had been hard at work on
Matisse for the last quarter mile, recalls, "We were always going
to win when Ken Coogan arrived on my outside going twice as
fast. He beat me by 1½ lengths but in another few strides it would
have been several lengths."

Helen and Des recovered from the shock sufficiently to dash
out on to the course to greet the highly delighted Ken Coogan
who gasped, "This could be one hell of a horse, he doesn't know
he's had a race." A few moments later, as he calmed down, Ken

added with stunning foresight, "What a hurdler he'll make."

At the subsequent impromptu press conference Des was asked if he had fancied Monksfield. He replied, "Not at all. Horses make liars of you, don't they?" Someone else asked how many horses he trained. Des raised a laugh as he answered, "I have a yard full of empty boxes." Monksfield, he explained, was only his sixth winner in two years.

Tote supporters of Monksfield that day enjoyed a surprisingly rich dividend. Anyone astute enough to invest 20 pence on his chances of winning collected the massive sum of £129.56, odds of 647/1. Two girls who ran the fruit stall at the racecourse entrance had £1 on Monksfield between them. When they heard he had won they threw their apples and oranges high into the air with gay abandon and disappeared into the bar for the rest of the afternoon. Another lucky punter, who bought a car on the proceeds of his win, was a teacher who worked for the Tote in his spare time. His identity must remain a secret for the two good reasons that he is not allowed to take holiday jobs and Tote employees are not permitted to bet on the Tote.

There was little time for celebration. Helen led Monksfield jig-jogging happily off to the stable area and held him while Des washed him off, allowed him to dry in the pale autumn sun, then threw a rug over his back and popped him back into his racecourse box where he immediately rolled jauntily on his back. Monksfield, certainly, was the least concerned of all that day at his unexpected triumph. Giving him a last, grateful pat Des rushed off to saddle Ettridge for the Handicap Chase.

Horse racing has been described as a frivolous pastime but it can also be the cruellest of levellers, one moment sending dreams soaring to the peak of ambition, the next plunging them to a trough of despair. Still bubbling over the success of Monksfield, Des and Helen climbed to the top of the stands for Ettridge's race and watched in horror as he was killed in a fall.

Monksfield's performance perhaps helped to ease the pain on the long journey home. Des says, "The death of Ettridge tore the carpet from under our feet. We thought he would make a top class chaser and, more important, he was such a nice character." They returned to Billywood with heavy hearts, one horse and an empty head collar.

When Sheila Mangan's mother rang Newfoundland that evening with the news, Michael Mangan had called in at the Golf Club on his way home from work. Sheila rang him there asking, "Do you want the good news or the bad news first?" Before he had time to choose she reported that Monksfield had won but her mother, advised that he had no possible chance, had not put on his £10 bet.

Michael Mangan laughs, "So you see ever since I've had this hold over my mother-in-law. We only heard about the huge Tote dividend later and, of course, if my £10 bet had been in the pool the payment would have been substantially smaller. I've been an unlucky punter all my life so I decided that as Monksfield had won without my support I would never back him again and I haven't."

Elated, Michael Mangan rang Des McDonogh later that night and stayed on the line for half an hour, discussing plans; but the young trainer, providentially perhaps, had not made any more entries for Monksfield that season because there were not any suitable races in the final fortnight.

Through the winter Monksfield thickened, grew more robust and, as has been his habit ever since, put on an enormous amount of weight round his middle. His leisurely holiday was enlivened by an occasional schooling session over poles ridden by Helen in a miniscule paddock. It might seem unusual to pop a 2-year-old colt over jumps at such an early stage of his development but it's a system that has normally paid dividends for the McDonoghs. Monksfield, it seems, was a natural. Helen recalls, "He was a great 'lepper' from the start. You could not get him to make a mistake and he never rose an inch higher than necessary. He loved it."

Within weeks of Monksfield's surprise victory at Punchestown his dam Regina was back in the sale ring. She had enjoyed a year off after Monksfield's birth but as she was barren after visits to Fine Blade in 1973 and Laser Light in 1974, the decision was taken to sell her. Arthur Ryan reasoned that her case was pretty hopeless. At that stage he made out an account and told Peter Ryan he was prepared to keep the mare while she was in foal, or rearing a foal but was not going to keep her if she was empty. Peter Ryan agreed Regina should be sold.

68

At the sale Arthur Ryan handed a typewritten note to the auctioneer stating that Regina had been seen to crib bite, then led her round the ring himself. Interest was minimal. She was, as we have said, barren yet again, an old matron of seventeen, and Monksfield's first win had passed almost unnoticed. Des McDonogh hoped to steal her cheaply but in the end she was knocked down to her greatest admirer, the redoubtable George Rogers, for 440 guineas. But poor George still failed to gain his reward for dogged persistence since, to Arthur Ryan's dismay, the auctioneer failed to read out the note about crib biting. So technically the sale was invalid. Ryan marched round to the sales office, who called in Rogers and told him about the crib biting. Did he still want Regina?

At this point the stories begin to differ. George Rogers is certain the deal fell through simply because Arthur Ryan would not give him a luck penny, the customary good luck fiver or so that is traditionally handed over by the vendor at sales in Ireland. Ryan disagrees and says that Rogers merely offered a derisory 150 guineas for Regina. Clearly the sale was off so the auctioneer's office then contacted the underbidder, no less a person than Des McDonogh. Would he like to buy Regina at the underbidder's price?

Here again the two versions do not tally. McDonogh is quite sure he declined the offer. Having failed to buy Regina in the ring, he had accepted the fact and preferred to look for another prospect. Arthur Ryan maintains that McDonogh, too, offered 150 guineas and believes, somewhat unkindly and quite incorrectly, that Rogers and McDonogh were in league. Whatever the facts of the extra-time dealing Regina, unsold, returned home to Inch.

Matters tend to take longer to resolve in Ireland than elsewhere. Haste and speed are unwelcome strangers in the Tipperary countryside. Arthur Ryan, says his cousin, is apt to leave letters and forms unopened and unsigned. Replies are rarities. So for several months the possibility of Regina's sale lay dormant until Arthur Ryan took the decision to send her to a fresh stallion, Flare Path. His wife had been pressing him to buy the mare from Peter, who had paid most of his outstanding bill. Before either of them knew if Regina was in foal to Flare Path,

Peter agreed to sell the mare to Arthur for £150. A fair figure, says Arthur Ryan, because that was what he recalled being offered at the sale and a sensible figure, too, since it just about covered Peter's remaining bill for the mare's keep. So Regina finally became the property of Arthur Ryan.

Shortly after the sale Regina was certified in foal to Flare Path and eventually produced a filly foal, Regina's Way. Arthur Ryan put her into training as a 2-year-old in 1978. He chose without hesitation as her trainer Des McDonogh.

He explains, "I'm not a great lover of trainers. I know too much about them to just put names into a hat and pick one out. Some gamble, some drink, some have far too many horses in their stable and can't know them all, some are doing it for money and some are plain dishonest. None of these things apply to Des McDonogh. He doesn't drink or smoke, is very dedicated and rides them all himself. He's certainly honest, a very nice person who has only as many horses as he and Helen can manage."

Arthur Ryan continued, "I think Des McDonogh's handling of Monksfield has been absolutely marvellous, because I know probably better than anyone what bad, second-class material Monksfield was when he bought him. If the horse had been a super mover with a bigger physique one could say any trainer would have done it. But the vital fact is that Des and Helen do 99 per cent of all the work and training. They were able to give Monksfield all the attention he needed. I'm sure if he had gone to a big yard we would not have heard of him again."

# 7

# 'The right man bought the right horse'

Anyone tempted to dismiss the form of Monksfield's first race as negligible would have been grievously wrong. The first six who followed Monksfield home that historic day all won the following year. Ardallen, the third, and Pink Palace, the fourth, each won four races, while Prominent King, who finished sixth, won five times in 1975, culminating in the Irish Cesarewitch, and was to meet Monksfield again both on the flat and over hurdles. Even two horses who finished out of the first nine at Punchestown won minor races.

The sole exception to this catalogue of success in 1975 was Monksfield. He ran no less than thirteen times on the flat without winning. Michael Mangan, anxious to see his horse in action, flew over from Newfoundland for his first race of the new season at Navan in April, stayed the night at Billywood and returned across the Atlantic the next day. He could not fail to be pleased as Monksfield, patently in need of the run, stayed on strongly to be third of twenty-five to Ardallen. The promise of that initial outing was not fulfilled, Monksfield was unplaced in his next three races and Ken Coogan advised Des McDonogh not to risk him again on such firm ground. Dr Mangan was due back in Ireland for his annual summer holiday early in June; the going eased a little, so the decision was taken to run at Leopardstown in an amateur riders' race over 1 mile, 6 furlongs, the furthest distance he had attempted. It was to be Helen's only ride in public on Monksfield and she is the first to admit she bungled the opportunity. Des, too, blames himself for giving his wife the wrong instructions.

71

The plan was to drop him out in the early stages and give him a chance but Helen overdid the waiting and let the winner steal first run. Monkey quickened magnificently but too late. He would have caught the winner, ridden by Betty Carmody, in another ½ furlong; even so he was a worthy second, staying on well. A valuable lesson had been learned. Clearly stamina was his strong point.

Monksfield came out of the race so well that as Dr Mangan was still in Ireland, he ran again 5 days later against a top-class field at the Curragh. Obviously hating the firm ground he was outpaced in the closing stages. As Des McDonogh left the stands he advised Michael Mangan, "That's it. We'll harm him if we run him on this ground again. We've all the time in the world."

While the horse enjoyed a deserved rest during the warm summer Des McDonogh rang Michael Mangan with the news that a bloodstock agent had offered £5,000 for the horse to be sent racing to Hong Kong. Despite Monksfield's slightly disappointing displays in the early summer his owner did not even

Michael Mangan poses proudly with Monksfield, then a 3-year-old, at Billywood.

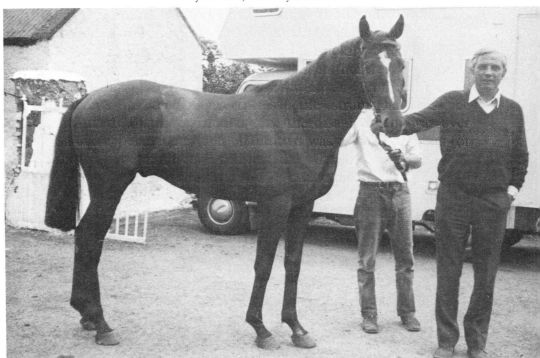

consider the offer. He recalls, "Monkey was far too precious to us. We hoped he might make a hurdler and were not interested in selling. I told Des to tell any further inquirers that the horse was not for sale at any price. If he could not win the Derby the next best thing was to take him to Cheltenham." No wonder Des McDonogh insists, "The *right* man bought the *right* horse."

The right man, Michael Mangan, was born shortly after his father, a doctor in Dunmore, County Galway, died in an accident. His mother, left with five children to bring up, bought a guesthouse in a field beside a church in Salthill, called Monksfield because it had once belonged to the monks. At the age of 8 or 9 Michael Mangan struck up a friendship that was to prove so vital in this story with a local character, Paddy Mulvihill, Des McDonogh's uncle, who worked as a transport manager and used to stay in a house near Monksfield.

The big event in the town every year was the Galway races, a 5-day spree at which fresh gambling and drinking records are set each summer. Mention to any sane person that you are thinking of spending a week at Galway races and their reactions are depressingly consistent. When I made the trip a few years ago Michael O'Hehir, commentator and bard of Irish racing, shook his head sadly as if my mind was going and my bank manager hinted gently that it might not be good for my health. In retrospect, the best advice came from Stuart Murless who trains on the Curragh. "As soon as racing is over each day jump into your car and keep going south as fast as possible until dusk. That's the only possible way you'll survive the week," he warned.

Michael Mangan, as a resident of Galway, had no such chance of escape and at an early age developed a deep and lasting affection for racing. He also inherited from his family, particularly his grandfather, a fondness for horses, dogs and all animals.

At school and university he was a fine all-round athlete, a strong swimmer, bold diver, powerful enough to become the Irish University Shot Putt Champion and a keen rugby and soccer player. His family followed in their father's footsteps. Four of the children, including Michael, studied medicine. The fifth became a nurse. Michael Mangan trained for six years as a doctor at Galway, acquired the nickname 'Hopper', and is remembered with some affection as an exuberant, sometimes

wild, but good-natured student. He completed a year's intern-
ship at Galway and continued his studies in America for a further
$2\frac{1}{2}$ years. While he was home briefly in Dunmore, helping his
brother, the local doctor, Michael saw an advertisement for a job
in Canada, applied successfully for the post and was sent by his
new employers to study radiology for two years at Liverpool
University. During his stay there he married his wife, Sheila,
also a doctor whose family lived in Galway.

On a trip to London to see the Rugby International at Twick-
enham between Ireland and England he met Jack Kelsey, a textile
manufacturer who lived near Liverpool. The pair soon became
close friends and the following year Jack initiated Michael Mangan into the delights of the jump racing at the Cheltenham
festival. The young doctor was an immediate convert. He completed his course at Liverpool and moved with his wife to a new
life in St John's, Newfoundland, but when funds permitted he
would fly over for the Cheltenham meeting in March. He admits
cheerfully, "I always enjoy Cheltenham even though I can't back
a winner. My money on a horse automatically puts a jinx on it."
Often he and Jack Kelsey discussed owning a horse. Once they
met the legendary Aubrey Brabazon, who in a golden spell of
three years, won three successive Cheltenham Gold Cups on
Cottage Rake and two successive Champion Hurdles on Hatton's Grace. Aubrey, by then a trainer, explained the finances
and pitfalls of ownership and invited the two men to his stables
next time they were in Ireland.

Jack Kelsey, thick set and heavily bearded, admits, "In a mild
way I used to try to dissuade Michael from owning a horse. I
pointed out he could buy fifty thousand horses without finding
one good enough to run, let alone win, at Cheltenham." There
was a more practical reason why Michael Mangan did not then
achieve his ambition to own a racehorse. As a young doctor, at
the end of a lengthy training, freshly married, his finances were
scarcely able to stand the drain of monthly training bills.

Matters, however, had improved by the time he met Des
McDonogh at Roscommon and now he runs the Department of
Radiology, where he both teaches and practises, at the Health
Science Centre, part of the General Hospital of St John's, New-
foundland. His wife Sheila specializes in eye diseases and they

Michael and Sheila Mangan in relaxed mood with their
daughter Maudie.                 *Credit: Henry Ponsonby*

live with their daughter Maudie, 9 in June 1979, in a split level
house whose cellar, converted into a Monksfield bar, is adorned
with racing photos and trophies of their famous champion. Tall
and grey, looking extremely fit for a man of 50, Michael Mangan
smokes incessantly, a habit he started when he would run all the
way to school and spend the bus money on cigarettes. He has
been a lucky racehorse owner, certainly, but has reaped the
considerable benefits of always putting the welfare of his horses
above all other considerations. A considerate man he wrote to
me in 1979 saying, "I would like to state that in my opinion the
patience, foresight and expertise of the McDonoghs made Monkey into the great horse we know today."

Back in the summer of 1975, while the sun continued to bake

the ground as hard as concrete, Monksfield grazed in the tiny paddock on the side of the drive during the day and was taken back to his box at night. Three sides of the paddock are railed; the fourth is guarded from the road by a 4 foot high stone wall. Flies have always annoyed him when he is out at grass. Sometimes he can be seen charging along flat out trying to escape their attention; he'll seem certain to crash through the rails then will pull up in two short strides. While Des and Helen were busy in the yard one afternoon they heard, in alarm, the rising crescendo of clattering hooves on the tarmac drive. Next moment Monksfield galloped round the front of the bungalow into the yard. He had jumped over the stone wall into the road, turned right towards Mullagh and forked right again up the 100-yard-long drive. Had he turned left the busy road led to Kells, Navan and finally Dublin.

Monksfield's holiday lasted $3\frac{1}{2}$ months. In that time Des took the opportunity to give him some much needed practice through the starting stalls. Most trainers have a replica set of stalls at home to educate their youngsters. Not Des McDonogh. He uses the partitions from his battered red horse-box as makeshift stalls. Staked firmly into the ground, with the entrance wider than the exit, the partitions serve their purpose well, as horses are led through them, first at a walk, then a trot. "I've never had one fail to jump out yet at the races," says Des McDonogh with justifiable pride. Monksfield was almost the exception on his comeback at the Curragh on September 20th.

The trusty Felix McCabe led him round the paddock that day, then joined the McDonoghs in the stand. When the race started Monksfield seemed to be in the pack. Then, to their dismay, they spotted his familiar maroon and white colours ambling out of the stalls a furlong behind the rest. Ken Coogan sensibly did not give him a hard race when he realized the cause was hopeless and shrugged off the incident. Ken thought Monksfield had summered so well that he had forgotten to fulfil his expected role. Felix McCabe voiced a more sinister explanation. His face crumples into laughter as he confesses, "I said at the time this fellow is a bit of a 'divil'. This boy is not putting it in. Sure we're all wrong sometimes. To think I even suggested 'Himself' was a rogue."

76

Five days later at Leopardstown Monksfield started on level terms but was disqualified from fifth place because his inexperienced young apprentice rider forgot to weigh-in. Des McDonogh was sufficiently encouraged, for despite erratic steering Monksfield had been staying on steadily at the finish. He then ran twice more unplaced over shorter distances, before tackling the Irish Cesarewitch.

Ten races so far on the flat over a variety of distances might not be considered the ideal preparation for a future champion hurdler. Des McDonogh agrees and points out, "We were learning together. The Curragh fiasco at the start was my fault because he was too relaxed, he had not run for ages. If I had a 3-year-old of his quality now I'd do things differently and a lot better. At this stage we hoped he would make a hurdler. He was such a good 'lepper' at home that in my mind I thought he would gain two lengths at every hurdle and that would be enough to put him bang in there."

Monksfield had only $7\frac{1}{2}$ stone in the Irish Cesarewitch over 2 miles and Des decided to reduce it further by using a young apprentice Stephen Craine, whose inexperience enabled him to claim a 7 pound weight allowance. Craine, from the Isle of Man, became Champion Irish Apprentice in 1977 and his career has continued to flourish. He was just 18 when he rode Monksfield in the Cesarewitch and had yet to ride a winner. His instructions were simple enough. He recalls, "I was told the horse stayed all day and as I had a light weight I was to make full use of it." Unable to live with the furious early pace Monksfield moved up steadily after a mile and forged into a clear lead with 6 furlongs left. Down the long, curving right-hand bend into the straight he was still in front, galloping strongly.

Craine remembers, "The others got to me 3 furlongs out but he was so tough, even when he was passed he ran on bravely. My whip had been *hopping* off his backside from 6 furlongs out and he never flinched, just kept going, battling to the line." Monksfield ran on to be third to Prominent King.

McDonogh was ecstatic. "I was over the moon. It confirmed he was as good as we thought and he stayed. Young Craine was very cocky. He came back and told me 'I thought I was going to win it for you, sor'. We thought so for a minute, too. It was a good performance by Monkey because he was still not furnished then, so much lighter and smaller than he is now."

Des tried without success to call Michael Mangan in St John's. Finally the jubilant owner rang at three in the morning. Des stumbled dozily from his bed to hear the unmistakable sound of a party in full swing at the other end of the line. "I remember the excitement in his voice. He talked for half an hour, was really bubbling and all the while I was exhausted, just dying to go back to bed."

Monksfield finished unplaced in his final two flat races of the season but that minor setback did little to shake the McDonoghs' growing belief that he had the necessary potential to develop into a very useful hurdler. Des frequently described his wife as the best schooling jockey in Ireland. Now that his leg had finally healed he was anxious to test Monksfield's ability over hurdles for himself in the bottom meadow. He was not disappointed. "Monkey adored it. He was like *lightning*. He got only the minimum height over his jumps from the word go," he reports.

Trainers like to school two horses upsides over jumps to give them valuable experience of situations and conditions they are likely to encounter in races. Des McDonogh did not dare adopt the usual practice with Monksfield. He explains, "Monkey was just too keen. You see, the last flight of hurdles in our meadow was within ten strides of the hedge and ditch and if he had been going too fast alongside another horse, well . . ." his voice tails off in uncontrollable laughter.

Des entered Monksfield in his first hurdle race, the Tara Maiden for 3-year-olds at Navan on November 22nd, a race that is always divided and hotly contested because there are so few opportunities for young hurdlers in Ireland at that stage of the year. As an unknown amateur he had won the race on Perplexed a few years earlier; she had been a brilliant jumper, had made all the running and he felt Monksfield was at least as good.

Bobby Coonan, seven times Irish Champion jump jockey, had noted Monksfield running well at the Curragh and mentioned he would be delighted to ride him when he started his new career over hurdles. Bobby had won on Ettridge for the McDonoghs the previous year and says, "I took Des at face value. If he said a horse jumped I knew he would not be

78

'codding' me. He always schooled his horses well."

Despite Coonan's obvious interest Des felt a little anxious about accepting the great jockey's offer. He admits, "Most of the time I was too embarrassed about the type of horse I ran to ask the top men. Naturally I felt they would be looking for a better ride. But Bobby Coonan was always a gentleman to us and I was more than glad to use his immense experience for Monkey's first race over hurdles."

Bobby Coonan is one of the survivors of Irish racing, a real man with twinkling eyes set in a ruddy, battered face topped by curly hair turned prematurely grey. Aged 14, light and weak, he had travelled to Epsom to start $4\frac{1}{2}$ years' apprenticeship with the stern disciplinarian Staff Ingham, at the not overgenerous wage of 10 shillings a week. "He was a great master and he taught me many things. I don't regret my spell there but it was a bit like penal servitude," he recalls. The ambitious young Coonan was given plenty of moderate rides but muffed the only chance he had of winning a race.

He explains, "It was in a boys' race at Epsom and I was beaten a short head, and a neck into third place. Looking back I should have won by three lengths. Staff Ingham had £1,000 on it and he never forgave me. So I only rode the bad horses after that. I came home to Ireland very disillusioned because I was after thinking I would be a Lester Piggott."

A brilliant judge both of horses and jockeys Ingham made a serious error when he sent young Coonan back to Ireland with a reference that read, "In my opinion this is a very good stable boy who will *never* make the grade as a jockey." Understandably Bobby Coonan was not in the habit of flashing that damning document in front of prospective employers for he was determined to disprove those cruel words.

Coonan describes his struggle to succeed in his own inimitable vocabulary. "It took three years of poking and rooting and riding screws, sitting on this, that and the other, but then I managed to climb out of the heap and eventually sat up on the top for a good while." His injuries over the years included several broken vertebrae in his back, dislocations, broken collar bones, broken wrists, arm and leg and concussion on numerous occasions. He dismisses that record of disaster with a flippancy typical of his breed. "As you can see *nothing* that was too serious!" Soon after he started training in 1977 his last fall proved to be his worst when he dislocated both shoulders, broke several ribs and suffered severe internal complications in a violent collision with a concrete running rail immediately after a hurdle. He's fit again now, is concentrating full time on training, and the light springs back into his eyes as he discusses Monksfield.

"Ah now, Monksfield, well he's a horse I would always be pleased to get out of bed at midnight to ride," eloquent testimony from one brave champion to another.

Des McDonogh missed Monksfield's first attempt over hurdles at Navan as he had to take two more of the stable's runners to Limerick Junction in the red horse-box. So Helen borrowed a trailer, hitched it to the back of their car, enlisted the willing aid of Felix McCabe and set off for Navan races just half an hour's drive away. When they arrived at the racecourse Helen jumped out and Felix walked to the back of the trailer to let down the ramp, mistakenly thinking that she was at the horse's head. Monksfield heard the ramp being lowered, tugged at the string securing his head collar and came charging backwards out of the box.

Felix McCabe will forgive me for suggesting he is not exactly built on athletic lines but he still moved with commendable speed in a desperate bid to catch Monksfield as he swung sideways out of the trailer. "It was a *terrible* moment," he recalls. "There were cars and lorries all round and the next thing he stood on his hind legs, about to plunge off, mad keen to gallop away and somehow I managed to grab a hold on his nose and the bob of his mane. Then off with him *round* and *round* in a big circle with me hanging on for my life."

His urgent cries for help were heard by Paddy Sleator's head man sitting in a lorry nearby. Grabbing a lead rein he dashed over to the scene of the impromptu rodeo and somehow managed to slip it over Monksfield's neck. "By jeepers I sweated that day," whispers Felix at the memory of the incident. "If he had got going he was a 'gonner'. He would have smashed into one of those cars and killed himself. Paddy's man told me, 'You may put your shirt on this today. I've seen this happen before and he's a certainty now.'"

Helen, meanwhile, had been chatting to her mother in another part of the car park, unaware of the drama and when she eventually returned to her car she found Monksfield, totally unconcerned, picking at grass behind the trailer with a shaking Felix McCabe clinging to his lead rein as though it was his life line.

The race was far less eventful. Bobby Coonan recalls, "Helen had told me he jumped super and he did. He made no mistake at all and I thought from three hurdles out there was going to be no problem. And there wasn't. Away he galloped and won easily on soft going. I was impressed all right." So Monksfield, third favourite at 5/1, won his first hurdle race, beating the useful Almanac by 1½ lengths with a huge field strung out way behind.

Fate dealt another cruel blow to the McDonogh stable that evening. When Des and Helen returned from their different trips they found to their horror one of their nicest yearlings, by Sovereign Gleam, dying of a twisted gut, that dreadful affliction for which there seems no cure. The yearling was owned by Larry McGuinness, a great friend, adviser and confidante, a loyal supporter through the darkest times. Their vet Seamus Murphy had done his best for the yearling but death was inevitable.

Monksfield wins on his debut over hurdles, at Navan, ridden by Bobby Coonan.　　*Credit: Irish Independent*

# 8

# 'We overfed him'

Monksfield was scheduled to run two weeks later at Fairyhouse. Once again the race was divided and to Des McDonogh's consternation all the good horses, including four previous winners, were in his division. Bobby Coonan had to fulfil his retainer for Paddy Sleator on King Weasel so Des booked Frank Berry, a wiry ginger-haired former star apprentice, who had won the 1968 Irish St Leger on Giolla Mear and was about to become champion jump jockey for the first time.

Favourite for the race at 5/4 was Troyswood, who had won the first division of the Tara Maiden Hurdle at Navan. Monksfield was on offer at 7/1. Frank recalls, "We won easy enough in the end but it was a hard race, against good horses and I really had to get after Monksfield over the last two hurdles. He jumped well that day but the thing that impressed me most about him was his toughness. He *loved* his work." Monksfield beat Troyswood by 4 lengths and confirmation of the form of his previous race came half an hour later when Almanac trotted up by 10 lengths in the second division.

Late in November the familiar figure of Joe Brady ambled up the drive at Billywood. Joe, aged 20, had been apprenticed to Cyril Bryce-Smith and had worked for three years with Des at Cherrymount before moving on, first briefly to the Curragh and then to Helen's brother John, training nearby at Trim. He gradually realized his ambition to be a jockey was hopeless and had drifted away from racing to work in the more lucrative building trade. After a few months humping bricks and mixing cement, Joe heard that Des was expanding his stable and wondered if there might be a job available. By then the McDonoghs were training nine horses, still doing all the work themselves, but Helen was expecting her first baby in January and Joe's appearance could not have been better timed.

Joe Brady started his new life at Billywood immediately and soon became a most valuable asset, but though he has led up Monksfield for nearly all his races he has never been the great horse's regular lad. That honour has always been preserved, most jealously, by Des McDonogh who mucks him out early every morning, rides him at exercise, grooms him in the afternoon and dotes on his every movement.

Des McDonogh, as you may have appreciated, is not an ordinary trainer. He acts as his own head lad, chief work rider, travelling head lad, box driver, secretary and most important of all, Monksfield's constant attendant. He feeds and waters all the horses himself, rides out a minimum of four lots each day and ever since he began training his unlikely collection of equine talent has maintained his occasional practice of leading up runners in the parade ring at the races if his small staff are stretched.

Joe's arrival gave the McDonoghs a chance to slip away to spend Christmas Day with his family in Limerick. Christmas 1975 was a time of unlimited dreams for them. Monksfield had won his only two hurdle races in exhilarating style and Michael Mangan was flying over solely to see him win at Leopardstown on Boxing Day. Already they were thinking ahead to the *Daily Express* Triumph Hurdle, the 4-year-old championship in March at Cheltenham, the meeting Dr Mangan had been attending for years with dedicated enthusiasm.

Frank Berry regarded Monksfield as a banker at Leopardstown in his cliff-hanging duel with Tommy Carberry for the jockeys championship. The pair were locked together on an equal number of winners with just two racing days remaining to the end of the year after Boxing Day.

Monksfield ran abysmally. Beaten at half-way, he hung badly and stumbled wearily over the line with only three stragglers behind him. Frank Berry admits, "He could not have run worse. There was no life in him, he had no interest at all. I gave him one smack but nothing happened so I accepted it. He was definitely *not* the same horse I had ridden at Fairyhouse."

Baffled and depressed, Des McDonogh could not understand the reason for such an uncharacteristic display. The horse seemed well before the race. The going was ideal. There seemed no possible excuse. Michael Mangan, as usual, took the defeat in good humour. He recalls, "Every horse runs badly in his career. They can't win all the time. As far as I was concerned it was a temporary set-back. Des thought at the time he might have had a sore hoof. At least my journey was not a wasted one for I saw Night Nurse win the Irish Sweeps Hurdle the next day. I thought he was the greatest hurdler I had ever seen." The young trainer still felt acutely embarrassed at his owner travelling thousands of miles for such a dismal show. Des worried and puzzled for over a year about that awful day at Leopardstown until a chance remark by Felix McCabe provided the answer.

"There had to be a reason", says Des, "because he's never run like that before or since. You'd *never* believe what happened. We overfed him," he confesses lamely. Felix, it transpired, had called in on Christmas evening to help with the horses and remembered Joe giving Monksfield a huge extra bowl of nuts because he was running the next day. When the McDonoghs arrived home from Limerick at 3 o'clock on Boxing Day morning, Des peeped over his box door, felt he looked hungry and gave him another large bowl of nuts. Four hours later in the cold light of dawn Monksfield still appeared to be hungry so Des gave him a further bowl of nuts. "In all", he says, "we must have given him nine or ten pounds of nuts on top of his usual diet. That must have been the reason."

Monksfield certainly ran a great deal better in his next race at Navan, finishing fourth in his first handicap on January 15th, two days after Helen had given birth to her first daughter, Shona. Four-year-olds have to take on older horses in handicaps in Ireland because there are so few other opportunities for them. Monksfield's next race was another handicap, in which despite his smart early season form he was allotted only $9\frac{1}{2}$ stone. Good jockeys are scarce at that weight. The choice was severely limited. Des did not want an inexperienced rider on the horse. He chose a tough veteran, strong and powerful, Tommy Kinane, a man who could do the weight with ease and was destined to ride Monksfield more often than any other jockey.

84

Tommy Kinane belongs to one of the largest racing families in Ireland. He's one of fourteen children and no less than six of his brothers are involved in racing. Dan, Christy and Jim all train racehorses and Billy, who works for Vincent O'Brien, led up the 1978 Derby favourite Inkerman at Epsom. Mick is box driver for Edward O'Grady and Tommy's youngest brother Ned works for him as head man at his rapidly expanding stables near Cashel. Three of Tommy's sons are already jockeys, so are four of his nephews.

When I asked if Tommy's charming wife Frances came from a racing family, too, he told me, "Not at all, women are only good for racing after flies." He lives with Frances and their seven children in a smart new attractively painted bungalow with a breathtaking view across the green fields of Tipperary to the hills of Slievenamon. There he farms 90 acres of his own, rents a hundred more and trains twenty horses in the most peaceful surroundings imaginable.

Life stands still in Tipperary. Old men in cloth caps lead donkeys and traps at snails' pace along leafy lanes past fields where sturdy yeoman in braces and boots can still be seen laboriously turning rows of hay with pitchforks. Crumbling high stone walls, riddled with ivy, guard ancient estates, once meticulously maintained, now falling into decay. Clutches of milk churns, glittering brightly, stand at attention awaiting collection. Here Tommy Kinane lives with his close-knit family in a forgotten corner of Ireland, where motorists lulled by the summer air and the sweet smell of hay are liable to be confronted on bends by herds of sheep or young bullocks, wandering aimlessly.

When I asked directions to his home, an ancient white-haired character, with the face of a choirboy, told me, "Kinane, the horsey man is it? Just follow the telegraph poles for two miles and when they stop that's where he'll be." He was.

Tommy Kinane's age has been the subject of endless speculation and the matter is not helped by the odd fact that at one stage he had three different dates on his birth certificate, the third, the eleventh and the twenty-first of October, 1933. His family now send him birthday cards on October 11th. The gaggle of Kinane children lived in a small house with an acre of land that was tilled to the last inch to provide food for the family. Cows, turkeys, hens and pigs vied for space alongside the highly productive vegetable patch. Tommy's father, a stone-mason, worked for Cashel council. His mother, he says, "was a great woman, but a contrary one and a lot of us take after her. Most of us have her fiery temperament. Father was a quiet man, very few of us are taking after him."

In the summer the family's cows would graze loose on what in Ireland is called 'The long acre', the grass on the side of roads. During school holidays Tommy would help his mother on their land and also earn a few pennies from neighbouring farmers by hoeing between drills of beet and mangles.

"My only good subject at school was fighting and I had plenty of practice," says Tommy, and the steely glint in his eye suggests he is not joking. As soon as he could he was away from the classroom, for the first year working on a nearby farm, milking cows seven days a week and snatching the odd half-day to go hunting. The farmer turned down his request for a free day to go to a local point-to-point but he cycled 14 miles to the races anyway, lost his 10 shilling note to a three-card-trick gang lurking near the entrance and pedalled home sufficiently impressed to take up an offer to work in a racing stable for Tim Hyde.

He spent two years with Hyde, gaining valuable experience as he rode work and schooled a variety of racehorses and show jumpers over all sorts of obstacles. The job folded when Tim Hyde broke his back in a fall from a horse called Heartbreaker. Tommy joined another trainer nearby and also encountered that perennial problem in Ireland, the demon drink. He admits, "When I was young I sampled *everything* and got drunk a couple of times. I did not like what I saw. I did not like the taste or myself when I was drinking it. I'd fight the finest when I was sober, I used to love a good scrap but when I had a drink on me I used to go quiet." He stopped drinking while still a young lad, has never regretted it and says now, "I don't like drunken people. I'd walk over a drunk in the road and would not bother to pick him up. More likely I'd step on him."

Tommy moved to England, working first for Tom Pettifer and then Tom Yates at Letcombe Bassett, the beautiful village just outside Wantage. He had a few rides on the flat in 1953 but was already growing heavy and left racing to try his hand as a scaffolder in London. Sometimes at weekends he would return to the calmer pastures of rural Berkshire to ride out for Tim Adamthwaite, who trained a big black brute, Arabian Chase, a horse that needed blinkers even to galvanize him into action at home. Tommy seemed the only person with the necessary blend of courage, patience and dash to ride this fearsome beast. Arabian Chase was entered in a novice hurdle at Wincanton in April, 1955 and Tommy began his career as a jump jockey on him since more experienced riders suffered sudden acute deafness when asked by Tim Adamthwaite to ride the horse. Tommy put up 2 pounds overweight at 9 stone, 9 pounds, finished nearly last on Arabian Chase and was pleased to receive his riding fee of 7 guineas.

While in London he boxed regularly on open air shows at Clapham Common and Battersea Park and also in club competitions. "I had many, many fights", he recalls with obvious relish, "and got beat as often as I won, but only just. The bright boys would keep running from me because I could hit hard. Lads would keep tapping away at me and running. They would want to box and I was dying to fight. Once I got them in the corner that was the end of it." He was unusually strong; his favourite party trick was to lift two men – one with each arm.

Tommy met Frances O'Brien, one of fifteen children, in London and discovered to his delight that she was the daughter of a neighbour in Cashel. A fervent dancer, he began escorting her to see the best bands in town. They married in December 1956 and returned to live in Ireland the following year.

His first ride in Ireland, three weeks later, was on Kilmore, who much later in 1962 was to win the Grand National ridden by Fred Winter. In 1957 Kilmore was a promising hurdler trained by Tommy's brother, Dan. "I rode Kilmore five times and you might say we had a few quiet runs together," says Tommy with a wink. "Then Dan rode him and he obliged all right at 7/4."

Tommy's first win came on his sixth ride in Ireland on Trade Union at Leopardstown on January 11th 1958. "'Twas a great feeling too. I did not know anything about riding a finish and he was a horse you could not hit. All you could do was kick like the

Tommy Kinane, after his first win as a jockey, on Trade Union at Leopardstown on January 11th 1958. He's pictured here between his brothers Dan, on his left, and Christy, on his right.          *Credit: Irish Field*

devil and hold on to his head and that's what I did.'' He's been riding winners regularly ever since, has survived some horrific falls, but late in the Autumn of 1979 seemed to be fighting a losing battle with his wife and children over his determination to continue riding in novice chases.

"I suppose they are right in a sense but there's nothing better than a challenge in a novice chase on a good 'lepper'. If I have a nice young horse I feel like riding over fences, no one will tell me not too.''

An intensely proud family man, fiercely loyal to his friends, Tommy Kinane is an amusing, good natured character whose occasionally abrasive personality has led to some unorthodox riding manoeuvres.

There was the time his great friend and rival Sammy Shields cut across his mount rather more sharply than he liked. Tommy sorted out Sammy with a verbal warning, "That's the last time you do that now, or I'll dust you some day, and remember what I am telling you." Undeterred the bold Sammy tried to steal up the inside of Tommy's mount a few weeks later at Dundalk. Tommy takes up the story, "I let him come to my girths then reached out and caught his horse by the bit and pulled his head in half-way over my knee. In the meantime Sammy was hitting me across the back with his whip but I would not let go. I kicked on to the next hurdle and just as I got there I yanked back on his horse's bit and he shot about 10 lengths behind me. Sammy gave me three lovely stripes on my back that stayed there a month, but I got the satisfaction of doing him properly."

Even the great Pat Taaffe, he of the soft speech and God-given hands, earned Tommy Kinane's displeasure. Pat, claims Tommy, barged over and almost drove him through the rails at Navan. "I told him afterwards I would do him the first chance I had. He's a real gentleman, but he had cost me the race and I intended to teach him a lesson. I got the opportunity of returning the compliment at Tramore a few days later. I arrived up along-side Pat going down the hill and passed him perhaps by half a length, then I looked over and called out, "Now, Pat, do you remember Navan?"

"Ah, Tommy", cried Pat, "you wouldn't?"

"I would not, good luck," replied Tommy as he quickened away to win the race.

Tommy admits, "I've had a certain amount of dust-ups with people in the weighing room but I would not hold a grudge with anyone. I would squeeze people up a bit all right but no jockey can ever say I've done any harm to them. Ever. We had a few very dirty, rough riders here but I was able to take care of myself with any of them." No one could possibly disagree with that statement.

Tommy Kinane, then, outspoken, fearless, amusing, a seasoned campaigner, began his long and eventful partnership with Monksfield in the Celbridge Handicap Hurdle at Naas on January 24th 1976. His orders were to hold his mount up and try to come with a strong run to lead at the last hurdle. He failed by a head, partly because the more experienced winner, Straight Row, jumped the last hurdle a shade more fluently. Tommy Kinane was delighted. He says, "I'd have won if I had really got after him. It was his first big test and he was brilliant for a novice against older horses. He felt a super, tough horse under me. Jump? He'd jump right out of jail!"

Monksfield had sufficient weight for Frank Berry to ride him at Navan next time. They finished fifth in a muddling race. Ten days later on February 21st, Tommy Kinane was back on Monksfield in another handicap at Fairyhouse. Once again his orders were to hold up his mount for a late challenge and once again they failed by a head to catch the winner, Bedwell Prince. Tommy Kinane was convinced he would have won if he had been allowed to make more use of Monksfield's undoubted stamina. Says Des McDonogh, "We talked it over for a long time afterwards and Tommy felt, quite rightly I think, that had he known Monkey was so tough and could take so much he would have tried to lead earlier."

Monksfield was already entered for the *Daily Express* Triumph Hurdle at the 3-day Cheltenham festival, the peak of the jumping year when the best horses from England and Ireland clash in testing conditions before huge crowds. Only enthusiasts need apply at Cheltenham. The facilities are appalling, the cost astronomical and the weather, in the third week of March, is invariably foul. But for true lovers of jumping Cheltenham is the only place to be that week. Monksfield's game second to Bedwell Prince had fully justified the expense of sending him to England and Michael Mangan, a regular at Cheltenham for years, was delighted that his colours would be seen there for the first time.

Monksfield's final race before Cheltenham was the Beechmount Handicap Hurdle at his local course, Navan, but a disastrous chain of events that overshadowed his promising career, almost caused his last-minute withdrawal. Early on Thursday, two days before the race, Des was called to Limerick where his father was dying. The young trainer set off at once with a heavy heart, for his had always been the closest of families and his father had been a marvellous supporter and friend. Clement McDonogh's death early on Friday morning was followed, an

Monksfield wins the Beechmount Hurdle on the day Des McDonogh's father was buried. Note the black arm bands worn by Tommy Kinane. *Credit: Irish Field*

hour later, by the death of a cousin in the city of Limerick. Distraught with grief, Des helped arrange both funerals for the next day, Saturday and insisted that Monksfield could not run. His mother eventually persuaded him to change his mind, arguing that his father would have liked the horse to take his chance.

Helen sewed black arm bands on to the sleeves of Michael Mangan's racing silks before setting off for Navan to saddle Monksfield. In Limerick Des McDonogh's spirits sank as he attended two funerals in succession, then sat in a car outside his brother-in-law's house to listen to the radio commentary on the Beechmount Hurdle. He did not wish to upset any of the relatives gathering in the house but discovered later that they had all listened to the commentary too. Monksfield's own brand of courage was needed that day to withstand several challengers in the last half mile. He won, all out, by three-quarters of a length from Notary.

Chaseform Notebook's Irish observer reported, "Monksfield

had to summon all his reserves to deal with a swarm of opponents from the penultimate hurdle and his handling of the second's challenge was full of spirit." Tommy Kinane recalls, "We came from nowhere. He got interfered with, knocked down, almost turned sideways. He never liked horses pushing him round, being in a bunch, and that day he just put his ears back and fought his way out of them."

Monksfield's gallant victory brought only the briefest respite to the mourners in Limerick. Two hours later Des McDonogh's mother was taken ill and rushed to hospital. Fearing she too was dying, Des collapsed under the strain and when Helen arrived in Limerick later that night he was barely conscious. He recovered sufficiently the next day to help with the family's arrangements and happily his mother, too, eventually returned to good health after her ordeal.

# 9

# Cheltenham

Travelling horses as air freight cargo can be such a hazardous business that the more nervous equine passengers have to be sedated. A 4-year-old entire horse, at the peak of physical condition, is hardly an ideal travelling companion, yet Monksfield, typically, took to flying at once. He walked into his box, glanced at the unfamiliar surroundings with indifference and dozed contentedly throughout the flight to Coventry airport. Des McDonogh waited anxiously at his head for the first 15 minutes, realized Monksfield was the most relaxed horse on the plane and moved forward to snatch a cup of tea with the crew.

Monksfield and his devoted trainer arrived at Cheltenham on Tuesday, the first day of the festival meeting, and when Des set out to walk the course he had only seen before on television he found to his consternation that the prolonged dry crisp spring sunshine had grilled the going to firm, an unprecedented state of affairs in March.

Cheltenham, 1976, was the start of a series of visits to the meeting by a group of Michael Mangan's friends and medical associates from Newfoundland. Falah Maroun, George Battcock and Galway-born Michael Maguire all accompanied him on that inaugural trip. Yet dinner that night at their Gloucester hotel was unusually subdued because they all knew Des McDonogh was seriously considering withdrawing Monksfield unless rain fell before the race on Thursday. Des says, "I will always remember being put at my ease by Michael Mangan. He told me that if I thought it was too firm he would understand if I took the horse out. That was a great relief."

Early on Wednesday morning Des cantered Monksfield gingerly over $1\frac{1}{2}$ miles round a tight circuit where light planes can land inside the racecourse. The horse seemed to stride out well enough on the fast ground and was so perky that he decided to run him. The rest of the day provided something of a holiday for Des McDonogh. He soaked up the atmosphere at this unique meeting, joined in the famous Irish roar as Dessie Hughes lifted Bit of a Jig home in the Lloyds Bank Hurdle and cheered repeatedly as Night Nurse stormed up the hill to a famous victory in the Champion Hurdle, ridden by one of Cherrymount's favourite sons, Paddy Broderick.

Night Nurse's owner Reg Spencer insisted in the moment of triumph, "That boy is as hot as mustard." Paddy Broderick has been called any number of names over the years since he set out from Mullingar but 'boy' is not a description that had ever been considered before. The silvery grey hair peeping from his crash helmet and his battered, boxer's face bore vivid testimony to a long and painful journey in a bruising world. But the smile was sheer ecstasy as he was carried into the weighing room on the shoulders of admiring colleagues. "Old Paddy," as they liked to call him, had been going round almost as long as Big Ben, but all the skills acquired along the way had been evident as he had dictated the pace from the front on Night Nurse, keeping just enough in reserve to withstand the scything late thrust of Birds Nest.

Des McDonogh found himself consumed with the emotion of the moment as he joined the rush from the stands to greet Paddy and Night Nurse in the winner's enclosure. Des ended the day quite hoarse but dinner that night was a far more convivial affair. Paddy Broderick's connection with the stable had somehow lifted the mood of the party and as glasses were refilled yet again, Des McDonogh, sipping his Coca Cola, began to think that Monksfield might even be placed if the going was not too firm.

On the morning of the race Monksfield cantered steadily for 4 furlongs, then sprinted for a further two. Before the race Des spent an hour in the racecourse stables grooming Monksfield, plaited his mane, brushed his quarters till they shone brightly, oiled his feet and arranged for Pat Healy, one of Mick O'Toole's stable lads, to lead him up in the paddock.

The field of twenty-three for the *Daily Express* Triumph Hurdle was one of the best in its history. It included the 4/1 favourite, Prominent King, winner of his only two races, including the Scalp Hurdle; Havanus and Tiepolino, two brilliant French imports, the tough stayer Sweet Joe, Soldier Rose and John Bryce-Smith's smart mare Mwanadike, successful already in three hurdle races. Monksfield was ignored in the betting at 28/1. The pace was certain to be furious so Des told Tommy Kinane to give Monksfield a chance early on, try to join the leading group sweeping down the hill to the third last hurdle and to save a little for the run-in.

Even so Soldier Rose set such a fast gallop that Monksfield was one of several horses struggling to stay in touch early on. As the field streamed away from the stands Tommy Kinane could be seen scrubbing and kicking to keep a position towards the rear of the main group. Monksfield began to improve steadily from half-way and as Soldier Rose faded running down the hill Ben Hannon sent Mwanadike into a clear and, many of us thought at the time, decisive lead of several lengths. For a few moments the race seemed over but then a small group headed by Monksfield detached itself from the pack and set off in pursuit. Jumping the second last flight Mwanadike was still ahead but Monksfield, Sweet Joe, Prominent King and Peterhof were all closing on her. Monksfield challenged on the outside but as the leaders rounded the final bend on the long run to the last jump Ben Hannon seemed for a few dramatic strides to be taking the wrong course. Mwanadike ran extremely wide, taking Monksfield with her, while Peterhof, Prominent King and Sweet Joe saved valuable ground on the inside.

"I thought", says Tommy Kinane, "that Ben was heading straight for his hotel in the town. I shouted at him to pull in but he would not." Even so Mwanadike still led at the last hurdle and Des McDonogh remembers thinking "My God, I'm going to be beaten by my brother-in-law."

A mistake at the last hurdle ruined Mwanadike's chance and suddenly she was swamped. Peterhof and Prominent King came through on the far side while Monksfield ploughed a lone trail tight on the stands rail. As the four raced up the steep hill for the line Peterhof's light chestnut head showed in front although he

95

The last hurdle in the *Daily Express* Triumph Hurdle, 1976. From left Monksfield, Mwanadike, Peterhof and Prominent King.                    *Credit: Sporting Pictures*

was hanging to his right. His jockey Jonjo O'Neill, immensely strong, a dynamic finisher, was hard at work with his whip in his right hand but still Peterhof continued to veer right handed. Tommy Kinane was indignant. He had just shaken off the attentions of Mwanadike and now Peterhof was gradually drifting across his path. He groans, "On comes Jonjo and for no reason he decides to have a go at me. He hung me up on the stands rails. He was right on top of me. They were trying to put me into the betting ring and they nearly succeeded."

Seventy yards from the post Tommy Kinane switched Monksfield left–handed to find a clearer passage. He did not stop riding. "As Peterhof came across I just pulled my horse's head over his tail with one hand." Monksfield ran on bravely to the line showing the spirit that has become his hallmark, particularly at Cheltenham, but even his limitless courage could not overcome the precious yards forfeited by the two incidents. He finished second, beaten 1½ lengths by Peterhof, with Prominent King staying on to be third just ahead of Mwanadike and Sweet

Joe. The first five finished a long way clear of the next group and the time was a blistering 8 seconds under average.

Tommy Kinane was furious but initially both Des McDonogh and Michael Mangan were overcome that their little horse had run so well. Several sympathizers advised Des to object to Peterhof and a few moments later Tommy Kinane insisted that he should do so. Both men felt their horse had suffered badly on the run in but Des warned Tommy, "We are in the wrong place to get the verdict."

Tommy Kinane and Jonjo O'Neill were called before the Stewards and Des McDonogh joined them to see the film of the race, both side on and head on, shot by the camera patrol unit. Says Tommy, "I was stopped in my run and told the Stewards so. You could see plainly how I had to switch away from the other horse's tail. I had to get the race." Jonjo O'Neill watched the film with growing alarm. He recalls, "I knew I had come across but we had not touched. It looked bad on film, particularly from head on, but if Tommy's horse was good enough to catch me there was room enough for him." The three men were ushered into a small waiting room while the Stewards considered their verdict. Des and Tommy by now were convinced they would win the argument while Jonjo admits, "I felt shaky about keeping the race."

The Stewards' decision to allow Peterhof to keep the race was greeted with disbelief by Tommy Kinane. He comments, "I was disgusted. Justice was not done that day. Anyone looking at the film could see what happened." Des McDonogh, wandering down to the stable area to groom Monksfield was not at all despondent. He says, "We should have been awarded the race all right but how could I be upset? I was over the moon; sure wasn't it fantastic to take just one horse to Cheltenham and do so well."

Michael Mangan, too, was overjoyed. He insists, "To be second – to me that was as big as the greatest victory in the world," and he arranged an impromptu party at the Queen's Hotel, Cheltenham. Des McDonogh was not there, since he had already started on the complicated journey back to Ireland with Monksfield. But when the horsebox reached Coventry airport news filtered through that the plane due to fly them out had broken down in Dublin. The horsebox turned round and headed back to Cheltenham and so Des walked wearily into the Queen's Hotel at midnight to discover the party was in full swing. A Coca Cola was added to the growing clutter of empty champagne and wine bottles littering the table. Several of Michael Mangan's friends had backed Monksfield, each way, ante-post, at 50/1 and Jack Kelsey, at least, had won enough money from the place bet alone to buy a broodmare, a three parts sister to the brilliant hunter chaser Credit Call. Jack named her Just Darina, after his wife, and in the Spring of 1979 the mare duly produced a foal by, who else, Gala Performance.

Des duly set off again in the horse-box with Monksfield at nine the next morning at a time when the last of the revellers in the Queen's Hotel were just going to bed, fumed impatiently all day at Coventry airport, did not take off until nine that evening and finally reached home, exhausted, at 2 a.m. on Saturday. In the morning, feeling shattered, he picked up the *Irish Field* and

Monksfield, ridden by Michael Kinane, just catches the odds-on favourite Masqued Dancer in the Halverstown Apprentice Plate. *Credit: Irish Independent*

saw an advertisement extolling the silk smooth, speedy efficiency of the company that had arranged Monksfield's transport to England. Shaking with anger he moved to his desk and wrote a critical letter to the paper which was published the following week.

Des McDonogh may have been tired after the tediously long journey but Monksfield returned in the most tremendous shape. Des had entered him in the Halverstown Apprentice Plate at Naas on April 10th because the race conditions suited him so well. Who better to ride him than Tommy Kinane's 16-year-old son Michael, just starting out on a promising career as a jockey? Apprenticed to Liam Browne, Michael had ridden just two winners and was destined to be Champion apprentice two years later. Odds-on favourite for the race was Masqued Dancer, who had cost 200,000 dollars as a yearling, had run consistently well the previous year and had not been disgraced in the Irish Sweeps Derby behind Grundy. He had the added assistance in the saddle of the dashing Tommy Carmody. Starting at 8/1 Monksfield beat Masqued Dancer by a head in a desperate finish. "He was so game," says Michael Kinane breathlessly. "He just kept at it and wore Masqued Dancer down. I was up against Tommy Carmody who was much more experienced but Monksfield would not give in. I've never ridden a braver horse." The form was made to look even better two months later when Masqued Dancer finished second at Royal Ascot.

Eleven days after Naas Monksfield took advantage of some lenient handicapping to win the valuable Huzzar Handicap Hurdle at Fairyhouse by no less than eight lengths from his old rival Bedwell Prince at the extraordinarily generous price of 4/1. Tommy Kinane reasons, "He was twice as good a horse after Cheltenham and is always at the peak of his form at that time of year. I took up the running a long way out and kicked on. Sure, he bolted in."

That superb victory, the easiest so far of his career, was his eighteenth race in seven months on all types of going. He ran just once more a week later on rock hard ground at Punchestown, carrying a big weight that included a 10 pound penalty, finished a highly respectable third and retired for the summer break he so richly deserved.

# 10

# Not for sale

At the end of their first season entire 4-year-old hurdlers, who have usually graduated from flat racing, are nearly always castrated (gelded), a practice carried out for a variety of reasons. At that age some of them will already be showing considerable interest in mares while animals bred primarily for National Hunt racing are normally gelded as yearlings, thus avoiding coltish behaviour later. A gelding operation removes the reason for that tendency, so enabling them to concentrate on racing without other diversions. Castration almost always improves a horse's temperament. They tend to become more tractable and maintain their form more predictably. Jack Colling, a most successful trainer in his day, was frequently quoted as saying, "Give me a stable full of geldings and I will soon have the bookies begging for mercy." There is another practical reason for gelding young jumpers. The very thought of banging certain parts of their anatomy on the gorse-covered top bars of hurdles would cause sensible horses to leap too high, too cautiously and far too slowly to ever win a race.

Dr Mangan quickly dismisses any suggestion that Monksfield might have been gelded. He reasons, "The horse had such a terrific temperament that the idea did not arise. I did not want to see him cut. He was eminently trainable."

Des McDonogh agrees, "There was never any question of cutting Monksfield. He never bothered looking at mares, he has always had the most superb temperament, and well, have you ever seen a horse try harder than him? He is a happy horse, in no way coltish. I learned at Cherrymount that if a colt took to jumping they were the best 'leppers' of all.''

While Monksfield was putting on his usual bundle of weight that summer Des McDonogh received an offer of £25,000 for him. The deal was suggested, inevitably, by Eddie Harty, a garrulous, highly entertaining character with his own hot line to the Blarney Stone. Eddie was a top-class horseman, good enough to represent Ireland in the Olympics and later spent a very successful spell as a jockey in England, riding first for Fred Winter and then Toby Balding. Tall and angular, he was a particularly effective steeplechase rider and won a string of big races including the 1969 Grand National on Highland Wedding. When a dreadful arm injury forced him to retire he returned to Ireland as a trainer with a difference at the Curragh. Every single horse in his yard was for sale at any time if the price was right. Swiftly the voluble Harty established a flourishing trade to England, especially for his old allies Fred Winter and Toby Balding.

"Commerce", says Eddie, "makes the world go round. I had spent years in England steadily building up trust and contacts. Even then I was trying to arrange deals. It's always been a business with me. If the offer is right I sell. I've got a family to rear, and you can't feed them on what horses might win."

Killiney was undoubtedly the best horse Eddie sold to England. A gentle giant, he was a brilliant hurdler, and developed into the most exciting novice chaser seen for years, winning eight rich prizes in succession before an uncharacteristic blunder caused his death on the most dismal of days at Ascot in April, 1973. Other useful Harty purchases include Snow Flyer, Decent Fellow, Carroll Street, Vulgan Town, and Overdose.

In the summer of 1976 Toby Balding was searching for a possible candidate to take to America for the new international steeplechase there in the autumn, the Colonial Cup, run at Camden, Carolina, on Mrs Marion Du Pont Scott's estate. She was relying on Toby to buy a runner for her in her own race. Toby Balding, a large, untidy, bespectacled figure, not unlike a giant teddy bear, with an unquenchable appetite for racing and life, was on one of his shopping trips to Ireland. Could Eddie help? Their choice narrowed to Mwanadike or Monksfield. A

101

deal to buy Mwanadike was arranged but fell through, so, crammed into a call box near Navan, they tried to ring Des McDonogh.

Eddie Harty comments, with masterly understatement, "The Mullagh exchange is not the best communication system in the world and it took an hour or two to get through." Eddie was thinking in terms of paying £25,000 but eventually the message came back that Monksfield was not for sale. Says Eddie, "We told Des that day we would like first refusal if the horse ever came on the market. In this business if you don't ask you don't succeed and it would have been a great coup to buy Monksfield. In America they like tough horses. I think Monksfield is a marvellous horse, trained to perfection. Horses to me are like women. They are all beautiful!"

Des McDonogh muses, "I was lucky to be in a position to refuse such offers. The right man bought him in the first place. Money has never been a consideration with Michael Mangan. He would not have sold Monkey for ten times as much." Monksfield, most certainly, is cherished by his doting trainer and admiring owner. Des McDonogh points out, "I would have lost him quickly if I had sold him initially to either of the two men who had the chance to buy him. Remember they soon took their other horses away." He paused for a moment then admitted with a rueful grin, "And I have to be honest. If I had owned him at that stage I would probably have had to accept Eddie's offer of £25,000, because we needed the money. Even we did not realize quite how good he was going to turn out."

By the time Eddie Harty's bid was rejected, Michael Mangan had acquired a half-share in Kavala, the horse who had started his relationship with Des McDonogh in such sparkling style at Roscommon two years previously. Kavala, an 8-year-old chestnut, had belonged to Helen's mother, but when she wanted to sell the horse Des bought him for £1,200, rang Newfoundland that night and passed on a half-share to Dr Mangan for £600. Once again the doctor had secured a bargain. A firm-ground specialist, Kavala finished third on his first run for his new joint owners in a handicap chase at Roscommon at the end of April, 1976. In the next 6 months he ran twenty-one times, winning five races, and failed to finish in the money only twice. He had already completed 152 miles under National Hunt rules when he started his annual winter holiday in October.

Monksfield was almost ready to do battle again at the time Kavala began his long break. As usual, he had thrived through the summer months. Des recalls, "Every autumn when I bring him in from grass I wonder how on earth I am ever going to get him straight. He always carries a lot of condition and has such a powerful backside you could drive a bus between the two cheeks." After several weeks trotting on the roads Monksfield began steady, long canters. Gradually he would lose the weight from his belly and put on muscle along his neck, back and quarters.

Three runs on the flat at the back end of the season helped bring him to fitness for his first race over hurdles at Punchestown where he came third on October 20th, ridden by Bobby Coonan, substituting for Tommy Kinane, who was out of action with a minor injury. Monksfield finished third again, this time to What A Slave at Navan, giving 21 pounds to the older winner, but he faded badly to be only tenth in his next race after being stopped at a vital stage. "I had probably been a bit too easy on him at home," says Des, "and when Tommy was baulked he saw his chance was gone and let him coast in."

Monksfield, no doubt, appreciated the considerate handling, for a week later he won the valuable Benson and Hedges Handicap Hurdle at Fairyhouse in breathtaking fashion. Set to carry 11 stone, 4 pounds, a large burden for such a young horse, he drifted in the betting to 7/1. When the bottom weight Ballymountain Girl surged into a clear lead at half-way, threatening to turn the race into a procession, Monksfield was the only horse in the race with sufficient courage and stamina to go after her. Under the strongest pressure he began to narrow the gap, had closed to within a length at the last jump, and produced a thrilling burst on the run-in to catch and beat Ballymountain Girl by 2 lengths.

"That", says Tommy Kinane with justifiable pride, "was the best race I ever rode. We went so fast all the way I was driving hard, stick up for the last mile. I had to throw everything at him going to the last, *everything*. Ballymountain Girl was still going well in front, and then landing over the last he suddenly changed into an extra gear and sprinted past her. I'll never forget how

103

hard I had to ride him. He was off the bit all the while to stay with them and then, half-way up the run-in, I had the whip put away and we were really flying."

The Benson and Hedges Hurdle persuaded Des McDonogh that a crack at the Champion Hurdle at Cheltenham the following March was no longer a forlorn prospect. Monksfield had shown in the best possible manner that he was still improving while in England not one serious challenger had come through to test the supremacy of the all conquering Night Nurse. Tommy Kinane, too, was beginning to talk optimistically about Cheltenham. "It was a bit difficult for me," he admits, "because as a light-weight jockey at that stage I had only had a look at a Champion Hurdle horse from a long distance away. But I thought his defeat of Ballymountain Girl was a champion performance." Monksfield's next race was his best so far at his bogey track Leopardstown, a course that has never suited his style of galloping. In touch at the second last hurdle in the Irish Sweeps Handicap there at Christmas, he was beaten for speed in the closing stages but still finished a creditable fourth, giving weight and age to the first three.

Des McDonogh's next ploy brought a barrage of criticism from racing journalists and rival trainers who continued to be baffled by his different approach. The weather had been so cold in January that Monksfield had been unable to do his daily quota of long canters. He was patently in need of the race when he finished fourth on Saturday, January 22nd, at Naas over 2 miles, 3 furlongs, so Des decided to race him again two days later on the Monday at Navan in another handicap for the excellent reason that he always seemed to do so much better on the second of two quick runs.

McDonogh's critics were horrified. The horse had his usual obligatory 12 stone, was set to give as much as 34 pounds to useful rivals, including Director General and some people were heard to say that if the trainer had set out to break Monkey's heart he could not have chosen a better method. But Monksfield is not a horse who can be judged by ordinary standards and he answered the campaign of whispers in the best possible manner with an exceptional performance, storming to victory by $2\frac{1}{2}$ lengths from Director General. The experienced trainer Peter

McCreery, standing by the last hurdle, came back with a look of wonder in his eyes as he told McDonogh, "The way your fellow arrived at the last he could have won with another stone."

That heartwarming triumph confirmed that Monksfield would be in the line up for the Champion Hurdle. He had run six times in two months, most of them in handicaps with lumps of weight, hardly an ideally quiet preparation for Cheltenham, and was to run three more times in similar races before crossing the Irish Sea. Des McDonogh is not alone in his criticism of the Irish racing calendar as he comments, "Unfortunately in this country we don't have anything else but these handicaps. The programmes are never changed from one year to the next. If you had a foal drop today you could pick a race such as the Sloppy Weather Maiden Hurdle at Navan in three years time and it would be held. There's no change, no initiative, no imagination in the framing of races to attract the top-class hurdlers. Only Down Royal put on a conditions race in which Monksfield does not have to give bags of weight to all his rivals. The Irish Sweeps used to be ideal, but that changed into a handicap, and even in the Erin Foods race a good horse has to give nearly 2 stone to useful opponents. It's a system that breaks horses. Many of them cannot take the strain of carrying all that weight so often in Ireland. But my horse is exceptionally tough, he thrives on hard work, has never had a hard race in his life. He has *never* been asked to do more than he could."

The Erin Foods Hurdle at Leopardstown on February 19th gave the McDonoghs the first direct line with the best hurdlers in England for the field included that grand old horse Comedy of Errors, twice champion hurdler, and still, at the age of 10, a top-class performer. Comedy of Errors, a warm 13/8 favourite, was set to give Monksfield, an 8/1 chance, just 3 pounds. They were both caught by the flying late burst of the unconsidered 20/1 outsider Master Monday, who sprinted clear on the flat to beat Comedy of Errors by 4 lengths with Monksfield 1½ lengths further back in third place. "That was a brilliant run for his age," says Tommy Kinane. "He can't, he just does not act round Leopardstown. He appears to be running away until we reach the third last hurdle and from that point you have to gallop left-handed round a long curving bend. He never seems to

105

stretch out while he's turning but that day he was running on up the hill the whole way, we were only just behind Comedy of Errors, and I knew we would be lengths better anywhere else than Leopardstown."

After the race Joe Brady led Monksfield back to the racecourse stables past Bridie's regular stall, a converted pram which offered such delicacies as chocolates, drinks, sweets and fresh fruit. Jig-jogging jauntily, Monksfield spotted some apples, dived at the stall, snatched one of the apples in his teeth and sent the pram and its contents rolling in the Leopardstown mud.

Monksfield's launching pad for Cheltenham was the Beechmount Handicap Hurdle at Navan. Carrying his usual 12 stone he finished third, beaten less than 3 lengths to Ballymountain Girl (10 stone), and Chinrullah (9 stone, 1 pound). Of those who finished behind them, Ballyross, King Weasel, Shining Flame, Cooch Behar, Double Default, Rathgorman and Owenius, have all subsequently won innumerable prizes, while Chinrullah has developed into one of the best horses in Ireland. Yet there is no mistaking the regret in Des McDonogh's voice as he reports, "We were very unlucky. There was a terrible schemozzle and we suffered more than anyone."

Monksfield flew to England on the Sunday before Cheltenham week, settled in well, and on Monday and Tuesday mornings worked steadily over 1 mile, 6 furlongs, ridden by Des McDonogh. Conditions could not have been worse. Persistent rain altered the going first to soft, and then to heavy on Wednesday, Champion Hurdle day. Monksfield is not suited by rock hard ground but equally does not like bottomless going. Night Nurse, the reigning champion, too, was thought to dislike heavy underfoot conditions. He had not run since being beaten by a neck in a triple photo finish at Kempton on December 27th by Dramatist with Birds Nest only a head away third.

In retrospect the most decisive moment of Cheltenham week came early on Wednesday morning as many visitors stumbled towards their beds in the grey dawn. Setting out from his hotel shortly after 6 a.m. the familiar figure of Paddy Broderick arrived at the racecourse stables to ride Night Nurse. Paddy's faith in him had remained stolidly unshaken through Tuesday's storms and gales which had threatened to wipe out the meeting before it struggled afloat. But secretly Paddy was worried about Night Nurse handling the glue-pot conditions. So with the aid of trainer Peter Easterby he organized an early morning work-out. "You see," says Paddy, in that slow deliberate drawl, "I had to convince myself the horse was back to his old self. Everyone knew he had been wrong. We thought he was on the mend but I needed to find out for myself." Squelching round under watery skies Paddy found, to his immense relief, all the old familiar power and sparkle in Night Nurse's action. "You could sense the horse was eager to race. He wanted to take hold of his bridle and he moved with ease through the ground," he reported happily before going off to breakfast.

As the rain continued to lash the course Birds Nest, a confirmed mudlark, was heavily supported down to 6/4 favourite. Two lengths had separated him from Night Nurse on fast ground the previous year and the drastically altered conditions seemed to favour Birds Nest, ridden by young Steve Knight in place of his regular jockey Andy Turnell, injured in a freak fall the previous afternoon. Master Monday was at 11/2, Dramatist at 6/1, and the brilliant Sea Pigeon generously priced at 10/1. He had been much fancied to win the race the previous year until a warble just under his withers caused his late withdrawal.

Sea Pigeon, bred in America, had been a high-class horse on the flat. Bought as a potential hurdler by a large, genial Scots businessman, Pat Muldoon, Sea Pigeon showed renewed enthusiasm for racing after he had been gelded, and at the time of the 1977 Champion Hurdle was invincible in handicaps. But he, too, was known to be unsuited by heavy ground and his jockey Jonjo O'Neill was filled with gloom as he paddled round the track that morning. "We made up our minds," he says, "our only chance was to go wide all the way searching for the best going."

Tommy Kinane, too, had walked the course, and found there was one particularly bad patch in the middle of the course on the approach to the last hurdle.

Once again Des McDonogh prepared Monksfield for the race, then arranged for one of Mick O'Toole's lads to lead him round the parade ring. In the last minutes before the off Monksfield was steadily backed from 20/1 to 15/1.

107

Paddy Broderick had resolved to make the running right under the rails where he hoped to find the best ground. Heading out into the country at a pace significantly slower than the previous year Night Nurse was tracked by Monksfield with Birds Nest, Beacon Light and Master Monday nicely positioned, and Sea Pigeon ploughing a lone furrow on the wide outside. Rounding the top turn the field seemed far too close to Night Nurse who had drifted ominously in the betting from 9/4 early in the week to his starting price of 15/2. Surely, we thought, the ground would beat him now.

Monksfield had been following Night Nurse all the way, jumping boldly and accurately, but running down the hill to the third last Tommy Kinane took a decision which may well have cost him the race. He explains, "I had a good position on the rails but other horses came up around me and of course, my orders were not to go on too soon and suddenly I was trapped in a bit on the inside so I had to wait to get out. I had to pull back a bit and round to get to the daylight on the outside. It cost me some ground but I made it up easy." In less than a furlong Monksfield tacked right across behind five horses before finding sufficient room on the outside. The manoeuvre undoubtedly cost him two lengths, possibly more, at a vital time.

Beacon Light came through to lead at the third last with his stable companion Birds Nest and Dramatist poised to strike; on the outside Sea Pigeon moved up menacingly with Monksfield. Now was the time for Night Nurse to fade quietly away but obviously he had not seen the script. Instead he jumped the second last upsides Birds Nest, while Monksfield and Sea Pigeon collided twice as they struggled to accelerate away from the hurdle. Beacon Light was beaten in a few strides, Birds Nest began to hang left, and suddenly Night Nurse was back in front, galloping strongly, tight on the rail of the final bend as Monksfield and Dramatist came through to challenge.

At the last hurdle Paddy Broderick asked Night Nurse for a final decisive leap and got the response he so badly needed. Alongside him, Monksfield, to Tommy Kinane's dismay, floundered in the bad patch of ground he had discovered that morning, barely rose at the hurdle and made a rare and most costly mistake. "It was," says Tommy, "the most expensive

A serious blunder at the last hurdle costs Monksfield his chance of victory in the 1977 Champion Hurdle. From left Monksfield, Dramatist, Birds Nest and Night Nurse.
*Credit: Sport and General*

blunder of his life and there was nothing I could do about it. It cost him his momentum, all his back end fell down, and it left me sitting backwards, a terrible position." A serious jumping error at such a vital stage is just about as deadly as a knock down blow to a boxer. But Monksfield has never taken a count in his life and now, like a persistent little terrier, he gathered himself for a counter attack. Scampering up the hill, his handsome head stretched out low, lifted by 5,000 Irish throats, he reached Night Nurse's quarters but the reigning champion would not be denied. Running on in the bravest fashion and urged on so effectively by his jockey with the looks and style of a battered policeman, Night Nurse drew away again to hold Monksfield by two lengths with Dramatist the same distance away third and Sea Pigeon a creditable fourth.

It was memorable stuff and though few of the vast crowd had

backed the winner on the day he received a tremendous ovation. For Paddy Broderick, too, it was a supreme moment in a career stretching back over 24 years as a jockey. Afterwards he announced his decision not to ride over fences again since he did not wish to risk injury when he had such an outstanding horse to ride over hurdles.

In second place Monksfield had not tarnished his reputation for indomitable courage. Des McDonogh recalls, "I was so pleased and delighted to be second. Although another chance had gone the horse had shown his tremendous character and Tommy and I could not speak. When I went out to meet him I was almost in tears. Even half an hour later we could not speak. It was sheer emotion for the horse. We knew then for certain he was a Cheltenham specialist and if he stayed right he must be there with a chance the following year."

Tommy Kinane, too, was overjoyed. He says, "Monksfield showed rare courage to come back like that. He's such a great fighter and never gives up. If he had been a boxer he would never have been beaten in the ring. But I think if I had taken Night Nurse on earlier I would have beaten him."

# 11

# Dead Heat

With his trainer once again doubling as his lad Monksfield returned to England a fortnight later to renew his rivalry with Night Nurse at Liverpool in the Templegate Hurdle over 2 miles 5½ furlongs, a race specifically designed by the new Ladbrokes management there to settle old scores from Cheltenham. The weights were framed to attract the best hurdlers in the land and had done so on the inaugural running the previous year when Comedy of Errors had beaten the brilliant globe trotting ex-New Zealand horse Grand Canyon by a short head in a stirring finish.

Night Nurse, the reigning champion was set to give Monksfield 6 pounds and their epic duel is regarded by many experts as one of the finest hurdle races of all time. But inevitably their race, like all events in the sporting world at the time, was totally overshadowed by Red Rum's sensational third victory in the Grand National less than an hour later. There was hardly a dry eye in the stands as he started up the long staring run-in with the world's toughest race already won. Emotional scenes in the unsaddling enclosure found his jockey and trainer, Tommy Stack and Ginger McCain, two hardened professionals, wiping tears from their cheeks. Those of us at Aintree that day, and the millions who watched on television, had been privileged to witness one of those rare summits of achievement that lift racing and sport far above its normally mundane pitch in life.

The 1977 Liverpool meeting was also important in the Monksfield story for the first sign of disharmony between his gifted young trainer and veteran jockey. The problem was not of either man's choosing. On Thursday, the first day of the meeting, in the Topham Trophy over the daunting Aintree fences Tommy Kinane's mount Glenvale Prince fell three fences out, giving him a painful kick on the point of his shoulder as they parted company.

Shrugging off the incident with typical bravado Tommy caught Glenvale Prince, trotted him back to the unsaddling enclosure and just over an hour later rode Kilcoleman to finish unplaced behind Sea Pigeon in a handicap. Early that evening his arm began to stiffen and by Friday morning he could not open his hand at all. Des McDonogh chose as his replacement Dessie Hughes, a man at the peak of his form with three winners at the recent Cheltenham Festival, including Davy Lad in the Piper Champagne Gold Cup. Dessie Hughes rode Monksfield early on Saturday morning in a brief spin with Davy Lad. As he dismounted he commented, "This horse doesn't appear to like the fast ground very much."

Des McDonogh, knowing Monksfield had improved since Cheltenham, replied, "Wait until you jump on his back this afternoon." The two men were still chatting at the stables when Tommy Kinane appeared wearing jodhpurs and riding boots, insisting he was fit to ride.

Tommy affirms, "By the morning my arm had come rapid well. I'd seen a doctor and taken some tablets to kill the pain."

The trainer was not prepared to take a chance. He had already booked Dessie Hughes and quite rightly felt Monksfield would need a fully fit rider for his rematch with Night Nurse in the afternoon. Tommy Kinane walked away in disgust.

Dessie Hughes was aware that he had not stepped in for an easy ride. He had watched Tommy Kinane many times chasing along Monksfield vigorously and had gained the impression he was a difficult mount because Tommy was fond of saying he needed two men on his back.

Dessie's orders were to harry Night Nurse, not to let Paddy Broderick dictate matters and to take him on in the final mile. Night Nurse was a shade of odds on at 4/5 with Monksfield priced at 7/2, betting that suggested a two horse race despite the eight other runners. So it proved, though the champion set off at such a furious pace that Dessie Hughes was at once slapping and

Locked together ... Monksfield and Night Nurse at the last flight in the Templegate Hurdle.

*Credit: Ruth Rogers*

kicking Monksfield to stay in touch. He says, "All the way I was struggling to hold on, pushing along, or I felt he would drop out of the race. Des had told me to take on Night Nurse but I was only able to do so because he made a bad mistake at the last hurdle on the far side, which gave me a chance to move upsides. He still had me beaten round the bend but he made a worse mistake at the third last and that gave me an even better chance."

Those two uncharacteristic errors laid the foundations of an unforgettable struggle between the dual champion and his persistent challenger; from the third last flight of hurdles to the winning post they battled heroically with never more than a head between them. Paddy Broderick reports, "My fellow stood off far too far at the third last and landed coming down on the hurdle. He had never done it before and it frightened the life out

113

of him so much that he became unbalanced and started to swerve going to the next hurdle giving the initiative to Monksfield. He did not want to take off but I got him organized, he jumped it well, and we were locked together from there to the line."

Head to head they fought out their duel in the sun, straining every sinew in their bodies to reach the finishing line. First it seemed Monksfield must win, then Night Nurse rallied. They met the last together, rose as one, and continued their clash on the short, heavily crowded run-in. Monksfield just appeared to have the edge in the final strides, but right on the line Night Nurse surged forward and no one in the enormous crowd, or watching on television, could name the winner with any confidence.

A tense wait followed while the judge called for a photograph to help him separate the pair. A few moments later he ordered an enlargement, while the Liverpool Stewards added to the drama by holding an inquiry into possible scrimmaging in the last furlong. Neither jockey was sure if he had won. Both hesitated

Inseparable at the line . . . Monksfield and Night Nurse dead heat in the Templegate Hurdle.

*Credit: Provincial Press, Southport*

outside the winner's enclosure but eventually Night Nurse's enormous band of supporters forced him in against Paddy Broderick's wishes.

Dessie Hughes, guiding Monksfield into the spot reserved for the runner-up, told an anxious duo, Des McDonogh and Michael Mangan, "I think I had him beat until the final stride when he came back at me. It's desperately close." Dessie was exhausted. He confirms, "I've never ridden a horse that was so tough, that needed so much driving. He was never such a hard ride afterwards."

Des McDonogh, pacing nervously, remembers, "That run-in. Oh, it went on and on. One minute his head was down and he was in front, the next the other fellow had edged in front. It went on for a lifetime." After more tense minutes the result of the photo finish was announced to wild applause. A dead heat. The judge could not separate the gallant warriors after 2 miles, $5\frac{1}{2}$ furlongs. Michael Mangan was so elated he caught his young trainer in an enormous bear hug. No wonder. It was the first time Monksfield's enthusiastic owner had seen him win. The bold doctor is a strong, powerful man and poor Des McDonogh felt he was being crushed to death.

Next came a further wait while the Stewards deliberated after viewing the camera patrol film of the race. Brave men they undoubtedly were, and honest, too, but even they would not have dared alter such a perfect result. Their announcement confirming the dead heat was greeted by further loud cheering.

Tommy Kinane, who had wisely passed up all his rides that day, made his way to the unsaddling enclosure to give his old comrade an affectionate pat. Now came the ticklish problem of the trophy for the Templegate Hurdle. Reg Spencer, Night Nurse's owner, and Michael Mangan, tossed a coin in the winner's circle. Spencer won and took home the engraved silver salver. Subsequently a second trophy was made for Dr Mangan.

After one famous victory Dessie Hughes set out less than an hour later full of hope that he might also win the Grand National on Davy Lad, but they capsized at the third fence without injury. Des McDonogh watched with tears in his eyes as Red Rum galloped to immortality and was then taken for a drink by the racecourse management. In a corner of the room, no more than

Tommy Kinane, who missed the race through injury, in affectionate mood with his old friend in the unsaddling enclosure. *Credit: Ruth Rogers*

three feet from a television set, was the forlorn figure of Brian Fletcher in floods of tears, completely overcome. Fletcher had won the National twice on Red Rum but had later been replaced by Tommy Stack. By the time of the 1977 race his career was over but the incident made a deep impression on Des McDonogh who, much later, was to face the same dilemma of changing Monksfield's jockey.

116

Monksfield returned to Billywood in the very peak of condition. He is at his best in the late spring and two weeks after Liverpool he ran in the Halverstown Apprentice Plate again at Navan, ridden by Michael Kinane, started favourite in a huge field of twenty-five, and won easily from Majetta Crescent, ridden by Joanna Morgan. By now Monksfield was virtually handicapped out of every hurdle race in Ireland but he was so well that Des McDonogh decided to let him run once more in the Downshire Handicap Hurdle at Punchestown on April 27th, carrying the crushing burden of 12 stone, 4 pounds. He was beaten less than two lengths into fourth place, giving the winner, Prince Tammy, also a 5-year-old, the astonishing concession of 36 pounds. Tommy Kinane was available that day but Des McDonogh preferred to use Dessie Hughes who had ridden the horse so well at Liverpool. It was a significant choice.

# 12

# The Prince

Soft-spoken Dessie Hughes, of the shrewd eyes and steady gaze, his hair flecked with grey, took longer even than Bobby Coonan to make the breakthrough as a jockey. His is a story of grit, determination and endless patience. One of six children of a Dublin postal worker he was fascinated by ponies on a visit to an aunt's farm in Wexford and declares happily, "It's been ponies and horses ever since. I can't remember anything I was good at until I started riding horses and I was not much good at that for a good long while either."

Tall and slightly built, he became apprenticed at 14 under tough conditions to Dan Kirwan at Kilkenny, a man who trained some thirty-five horses and employed a minimal staff. The most experienced lads there warned Dessie Hughes he would be wise not to stay, but the more they chipped away at his confidence the more he was determined to persevere.

"It was very hard," he concedes. "I was the youngest there, was not very strong then, and we would work all day from seven in the morning until six at night. Six of us rode out at least six lots every day but Dan Kirwan kept his promise to give me rides and I think that was the only reason I stayed." At the time Kirwan trained a nice, young grey chaser Nicolaus Silver. "He was the most lovely jumper," says Dessie. "You never saw him make a mistake in his life." Dessie still remembers feeling disappointed when Nicolaus Silver was sent to the Goffs November sales where he was bought by Fred Rimell for a give-away price of 2,500 guineas. Less than five months later he became the second of that great trainer's four Grand National winners.

From six rides for Kirwan, Dessie was second twice, including a narrow defeat at Mallow, in 1959, when as a raw, inexperienced 15-year-old weighing under 7 stone he was just beaten on a filly who jumped pools of water lying under the stands rails.

Soon after Dan Kirwan died Dessie Hughes' indentures were transferred to Willie O'Grady, a clever trainer whose methods were more efficient and included a regular daily timetable for the lads. Dessie rode his first winner for O'Grady on Sailaway Sailor twice in three days, the first time in a 1½ mile flat race at Tramore. Sailaway Sailor was a 7/1 chance in a field of six runners but in a hectic finish scrambled home by a neck from the 2/1 favourite Duffcarrig, ridden by Pat Taaffe and trained by Tom Dreaper, the marvellously gifted pair who had reached the pinnacle of their lives with the legendary Arkle.

Dessie's triumph lasted until the Stewards disqualified Sailaway Sailor. He explains, "I left the rails in the straight and cut off Pat when he tried to come up my inside, so he had to switch round me. Even so I was still very upset at losing the race and it must have showed on my face because Pat came up, apologized for objecting and slipped me £2."

The Stewards held such a dim view of Dessie Hughes' steering that they took the harsh decision to place Sailaway Sailor last. Willie O'Grady, however, did not agree with their judgement and proved his faith in his eager young jockey by allowing him to ride the same horse again three days later at Ballinrobe on June 14th 1962, in another staying handicap. This kind, thoughtful gesture by O'Grady gained its deserved reward when Sailaway Sailor and Dessie Hughes duly won by 2 lengths. The wide difference between the lifestyles of jockeys and stable lads was spelled out for the first time to Dessie Hughes that night. Until then he had always travelled to and from the races in O'Grady's ancient horse-box. After his victory at Ballinrobe Willie O'Grady told him, "You are going home in the car with me." On the way they stopped off for a meal with some of Willie's owners and arrived at the stables late at night. The next morning Dessie Hughes brushed the yard with renewed vigour.

In the subsequent two years Dessie's weight shot up from 8 to 10 stone. His brief flurry on the flat was clearly over. He stayed with O'Grady after his apprenticeship ended, schooling young

119

horses frequently over hurdles and fences and won a minor handicap chase on Baxier. Good rides were scarce and his chief rival in the yard, Stan Murphy, seemed to be getting the pick of them, so Dessie moved on, spent a year with George Wells and then answered an advertisement in the *Irish Field* to work in Scotland for Eugene Ferris, who combined running an hotel at Lockerbie with training a small string of racehorses. Ferris had such a demanding daily routine that the horses pulled out between 5 and 6 o'clock and galloped in the dark behind the trainer in his Land-Rover showing the way with his headlights. It was a friendly, neat yard and often Dessie Hughes had finished the morning's work by 9 o'clock. He rode four winners for Ferris but after a chance success on Ocho Rios at far away Towcester over the Whitsun Bank Holiday he decided to move south to join that horse's trainer Reg Akehurst.

Dessie explains, "I was very ambitious. I always thought in my head I'd make a jockey one day, some day. Progress was very slow. I made mistakes. I think I always tried too hard and didn't relax sufficiently in a race. Eugene was very good to me, and we still keep in touch, but it was so cold in Scotland, so I moved to Reg who was then training near Basingstoke." It proved a disastrous switch. In a complete season with Reg Akehurst Dessie Hughes failed to achieve a single win. He says, "I know I was not a very good jockey but Reg had some terrible horses then, some desperate hairy things."

On March 14th 1966, he rode Willow Red, a complete outsider in a poor maiden hurdle at Wolverhampton, in a field of twenty-nine, certainly too many for that course's tight bends. Willow Red was with the leaders when he was brought down by another faller at the second hurdle, plunging his jockey on to his back facing the obstacle that had just caused his downfall. Twenty or so runners thundered past, hooves pounding and one landed right on Dessie Hughes' chest. He spent the next three months in hospital, lingering painfully while doctors puzzled about the nature of the injury. Constant tests, X-rays, injections and examinations failed to diagnose his problem. Doctors muttered vaguely about tuberculosis or other lung diseases. Reg Akehurst had only just moved to Russley Park, near Baydon, in Wiltshire, and Dessie had not had any time to make any friends there. He languished in Swindon Hospital, alone, miserable, depressed, certain he would not ride again, in constant pain, worried about his health, fortified only by the daily visits of his fiancée Eileen, who had moved to the area to be near him.

Finally he was sent to Churchill Hospital, Oxford, where a specialist looked at fresh X-rays and told him breezily, "I can see what's wrong. I'll arrange for you to be brought back here next week when I'll operate and put you right." The surgeon had to take away a rib first so that he could remove blood clots on the lung that had been punctured in the fall.

The operation left a huge scar on his chest, the shape of a giant horse-shoe, but within 10 days Dessie was able to return home to Dublin to recuperate with his family. A lesser man would have left racing for good. He had little to show for nine years of dedication bar a handful of winners, several painful falls, an aching body, an empty bank account and severely dented pride. But he was still determined to be a jockey. After a month at home he had recovered enough to work for Mick Byrne breaking in young horses at his stables near Phoenix Park, Dublin. While he was there he rode a winner for another trainer on a spare ride in a claiming lads race at Leopardstown. The flame of ambition was still flickering.

Dessie met Mick Byrne's nephew Mick O'Toole, a round, jolly, gifted greyhound trainer, once a butcher, whose amiable patter concealed a cool brain. Mick O'Toole was beginning to train a few horses as well as greyhounds at Ashtown, near Castleknock on the edge of Phoenix Park and had just landed the most ferocious gamble on a horse called Lintola at Edinburgh. Dessie joined him, initially as head lad. So began one of the most successful partnerships in Irish racing; Mick O'Toole, imaginative, ambitious, a gambler with a flair for publicity, and the necessary courage to buy batches of horses without a prospective owner in sight; and Dessie Hughes, the quiet man of the two, an honest, hard-working support, rock solid, with an instinctive knowledge of horses and still a desire to be a successful jockey.

Mick O'Toole's stable at Ashtown was soon overflowing with horses so he began searching for larger, more suitable accommodation on the edge of the Curragh. One day he and

121

Dessie inspected the Athgarvan Stud, on the market for £28,000. It seemed an ideal setting but was just too far from the Curragh gallops, so they looked elsewhere. In 1979, the Athgarvan Stud was sold again for close on half a million pounds ... such is the rapid inflation in Ireland. Mick O'Toole eventually chose Maddenstown, a small stable, with scope for expansion, close to the Irish National Stud.

Dessie Hughes bought a mobile home, married Eileen and moved into the yard. He lived there for a year, working by day and on the spot at night. Eventually Mick O'Toole built an impressive bungalow on a hillock overlooking his new empire and Dessie bought a house nearby when Eileen was expecting their first child.

Mick O'Toole now has one hundred immaculate brightly painted boxes at Maddenstown, with neatly kept flowerbeds in the main yards and a vast covered indoor ride, a furlong round. In the summer of 1979 those hundred or so boxes were overflowing with horses in training, the best of them being Dickens Hill, winner of the Irish 2,000 Guineas and the Eclipse Stakes, and runner-up in the English and Irish Derbys. Mick admitted to having another hundred horses either out to grass, or dotted around the countryside, yearlings, or older unbroken prospects and dozens of jumpers waiting to come into training in the autumn.

Dessie Hughes comments, "I've never known anyone remotely like Mick. He's a great thinker, can mix with anyone and his great secret is his adaptability. He'd come home with ten horses from the sales and would not sell them until they were broken, being ridden and going well enough for him to see a spark in them. If they were no good he would get rid of them himself, often five or six at a time in one lot to a horse dealer." As the stable progressed so Dessie began to ride winners frequently. Mick O'Toole started his famous raids on Cheltenham in the early 1970s and his first winner there, Davy Lad in the 1975 Sun Alliance Novice Hurdle, was, of course, ridden by the reliable Dessie Hughes. It was a triumphant return to England for the man whose initial steps on the racing ladder there had been so painful.

Even so Dessie prefers riding in England. He explains, "You

Dessie Hughes. *Credit: George Selwyn*

have an easier chance of riding a sensible race there. At home every jockey wants to be second or third on the inside," he laughs, "as a matter of fact that's where I prefer to be and the trouble is there are usually six or eight fellows all trying to be in the same place on the rail. So there can be up to nine horses taking up the inside and none at all on the outside. You have to be right on your toes to avoid being stopped or messed about. In England they spread out . . . if you want to be in a certain position you can do it."

Dessie's long, eventful partnership with Mick O'Toole ended early in 1979 when he decided to train on his own. All his riding fees and earnings had gone towards building a smart yard with

123

twenty-four boxes, two hay barns, a tack room and a further almost completed yard standing on 5½ acres behind his small bungalow at Brownstown at the edge of the Curragh. In February, 1979, he put Brownstown on the market and bought Osborne Lodge, an established racing stable with forty-five boxes, a house and 31 acres close to the 6 furlong starting gate on the Curragh racecourse.

Dessie Hughes' extraordinary relationship with Mick O'Toole is perhaps best summed up by an intriguing story told by a friend of both men, John Mulhern, a high-powered businessman, who early in 1973 had been persuaded by Mick O'Toole to pay 8,000 guineas, rather more than he wanted, for a promising young horse Kelly's Hero. O'Toole silenced Mulhern's grumbles by promising he would get his money back and more the first time the horse was fancied.

Mulhern, appropriately enough, rode Kelly's Hero, carrying several pounds overweight, to finish in midfield in a Madhatters Private Stakes, a fun race for enthusiasts, eccentrics and comedians held at Phoenix Park in July, 1973. Mulhern wore his own bizarre racing colours, a red jacket with a large white question mark on the front and the back, which caused one wag to pose the question: "If the jockey does not know if he's trying what chance does the poor punter have?"

Two months later Mick O'Toole rang Mulhern to tell him Kelly's Hero was running at Limerick Junction the following day. Says John, "Mick explained he had to attend the sales and assured me Kelly's Hero was not ready and could not possibly win. But he did tell me his horse Bit of a Jig was a certainty in an earlier race and that Paddy Sleator's Lucy Swan would win my race."

Armed with this useful information John travelled to Limerick Junction with Dessie Hughes and won a monkey (£500) on Bit of a Jig. He recalls, "I had the ammunition so before the last race I walked into the betting ring, saw Kelly's Hero was drifting in the market and put the whole £500 on Lucy Swan before hurrying to the parade ring to see my horse."

In the paddock poor Mulhern stood totally bemused as he heard Dessie Hughes, who saddled Kelly's Hero in the absence of the trainer, give amateur jockey Bob Townend his instructions. John recalls incredulously, "Dessie told Bob to be in the front three all the way and at the final turn to give Kelly's Hero two or three round the tail board and go as hard for home as he could and be sure to win."

White faced John Mulhern caught Dessie Hughes by the arm and croaked, "Now hold on, Dessie, there must be some mistake here?"

Dessie Hughes replied, "Not at all. Those are my orders from the boss and he says I am to take you straight up to the stands without going near the bookies."

Mulhern, fearing his £500 was on a loser, managed to slip his companion and headed for the ring intending to have a large saver on Kelly's Hero. But before he reached there a hand from behind gripped his arm as fiercely as an iron vice. Dessie Hughes whispered, "Please do as Mick says."

Reluctantly John Mulhern allowed himself to be led, somewhat forcibly, to the stands, where, with a mixture of horror and rising anger he saw Kelly's Hero sweep home by six lengths with Bob Townend looking round for non-existent dangers. Close to a seizure John leaned for support on a rail and recovered from the shock sufficiently to gasp, "Dessie. What in the hell is going on? The blood is pouring out of my body. I've done all my money and told all my friends the horse was not fancied."

Dessie Hughes shook his head as he replied, "I don't know but we are to meet the boss tonight for a drink." On the way home from Limerick Junction John Mulhern was inconsolable. Deflated, depressed, out of pocket, he mumbled bitterly to himself in the back of the car. Finally they reached the hotel where they were due to meet the trainer.

John Mulhern takes up the story. "There was the big man, Micko, smiling all over his face in the lobby. Before I could get in a blow he said, 'Well done. Didn't I promise you would get your money back and more? I've had a grand (£1,000) on for you at the best price and some for myself and the only one that knows is Dessie. So you've got your £8,000 back and more. Are you happy now? If I'd told you before and you had let all your friends in the know we would only have had 6/4.' "

John Mulhern concludes with total admiration, "Mick is a genius but Dessie, he's a Prince."

# 13

# A very independent person

Monksfield spent the summer of 1977 on his own in his custom-ary small paddock on the side of the drive. He would pick contentedly at grass in the day and devour his usual diet of nuts and hay in his box in the evenings, for Des McDonogh continues to feed him copious amounts of racehorse nuts in the summer months, reasoning, "We continue to eat well when we go on holiday so why shouldn't he?" There was one ludicrous change to his summer arrangements in 1977. Dr Mangan, home with his wife Sheila in his native Dunmore, could not possibly refuse a request from the town's festival committee for Monksfield to parade there.

Parading thoroughbred racehorses in confined spaces can be a tricky business. Red Rum, it is true, has already made more from his numerous public appearances than he earned in 10 years of honest endeavour on the racecourse. He travels the length and breadth of Britain in his own personal luxurious horse-box, raising attendances by thousands wherever he goes. 'Rummy' has opened pubs, clubs and supermarkets, turned on the Black-pool illuminations, kicked off football matches and on one occasion, made a startling guest appearance on the dance floor at an exclusive dinner held on the sixth floor in one of London's smartest West End hotels. But there is one vital difference between Red Rum and Monksfield. 'Rummy' is a gelding while the latter is a highly charged stallion who will eventually take up his duties at stud. So it was with some trepidation that Des McDonogh set off to drive Monksfield to Dunmore in the familiar red horse-box.

126

The plan was for Monksfield to head the parade through the narrow streets of Dunmore, led by his proud owner and ridden in racing silks by his anxious trainer, who observes drily, "You've probably noticed everything is late starting in Ireland and the Dunmore procession was no exception. Monkey looked fantastic but he began to get impatient and knocked lumps out of the side of a wall. The main street was black with people and he was absolutely mad as a hatter."

The thousands packing the route gave Monksfield a warm ovation and the cheering reached a new crescendo as Michael Mangan led his great horse into the main square. Des McDonogh, clinging tightly to Monksfield's back, remembers, "He was prancing and going and then when we were right in the centre of the square, Holy God, he threw one of his big ripping bucks in front of the platform where the dignitaries were sitting."

Monksfield returned to Billywood unscathed and his trainer was glad when the time came at the beginning of August to start the meticulously planned programme that would end, he hoped, with victory in the 1978 Champion Hurdle. Monksfield's training routine has altered considerably since his first buoyant steps as a 2-year-old. Gradually he has needed more and more long steady work at home to reach and maintain peak fitness. "If you put together all the mileage he has done at home I'm quite convinced it would stretch from here to America and back again," says Des McDonogh. "He needs a fantastic amount of regular cantering before he is even remotely fit."

His schedule starts each year, early in August, like most jumpers fresh from grass, with daily walking and trotting on the roads for an hour or so. Road work helps disperse excess fat, tightens muscles and most important of all hardens legs which have been inactive in the summer. After a month's exercise on the roads Monksfield begins steady cantering, over short distances initially, but later, as he became fitter, building up to two, sometimes three miles each day.

"He loves his work," says Des McDonogh, with ill-concealed pride. "I've never known him say 'No' to work, racing or anything. If he was a human being he would be far too willing to be a trade unionist. He's a very independent person, relishes his

127

work, and enjoys his grub and his sleep. Most of all he loves his sleep.''

I have to report that Monksfield's sleeping habits are not popular with the McDonoghs' two young daughters whose bedroom is only yards from his box. The simple fact is that he is the noisiest imaginable snorer, so loud that at night he sometimes wakes the little girls. Once Michael Mangan, in distant Newfoundland, could hear the snoring as Des McDonogh held the telephone towards the horse's box.

Autumn is a welcome season for Des McDonogh as it heralds the resumption of his partnership with his favourite horse after the summer break. He relishes the time he spends in Monksfield's box, grooming, brushing, sometimes just talking. He admits, ''I could quite happily stay out there for an hour each evening chatting away to him. You may think I'm mad but I'm convinced he understands what I say. He takes longer to do over in the evening than any other horse in the yard even though he is small. His rear end, for instance, is twice as wide as any other, twice as long, you see he has the most beautiful quarters. It's a treat for me to be in his box. Monksfield is the first person I see in the morning and the last I see at night. On the worst days he puts us in good humour. I've been his lad from the word go and the boys in the yard cannot understand why I don't let one of them take over. Most trainers, too, think I'm a bloody fool to do so many jobs but I enjoy it. When you are not really in the top league the economics demand you do the work yourselves. I don't think I could be a party to training from the sitting room, the study or the office, merely supervising the gallops from a car window. I like to ride them. Helen is the same. We must be involved and we find out far more by riding out every morning.''

Partnered by his trainer Monksfield does a prodigious amount of work but Des McDonogh emphasizes that he does not allow his horses to gallop flat out at home. He insists, ''The vast majority of Monkey's work is at half-speed, three-quarters maybe at the finish. He pulls a nice bit at home and can do half-speeds for long spells. For the first half-mile he won't do much, then he gradually builds up momentum. I've never known a horse need anything like so much steady work. I could not give him too much.''

128

The plough circuit of Monksfield's early days at Billywood had long been abandoned because it contained too many stones and the stable's first all-weather gallop had been swept away in a deluge of winter rain. In the summer of 1977 Des McDonogh began to build a new all-weather sand gallop with the help of Felix McCabe and another friendly neighbour, Cecil Carolan. They pushed out a hedge, merged two fields into one and dug down to a hard-core base for the gallop, half a mile round. Sand delivered at £60 a load from Drogheda was spread to a uniform level almost a foot deep. It was a vital addition to the training facilities, particularly useful in the summer months when the land elsewhere on the farm baked hard, even cracked in places.

In full training Monksfield's weekly routine starts on Monday with steady cantering at any distance from two to three miles. On Tuesday he moves into strong work over 1 mile, 6 furlongs. Wednesday will find him on the roads, for three or four miles, walking, trotting and cantering. "Cantering," I asked incredulously? "Isn't that dangerous on the roads? Do you put knee boots on him?"

"Not at all," laughs Des McDonogh. "Sure he's a celebrity round here and the locals are waiting to see him in their cars. We canter four or five of us in single file up this particular hill for three-quarters of a mile. It's the best hill in Ireland to get a horse fit and perfectly safe." Just once a lorry came over the brow of the hill, going too quickly. Helen was in the lead and her mount, taking fright, slid to the ground, happily without injury to either of them.

On Thursday and Saturday Monksfield canters steadily again over long distances. Friday is reserved for more fast work. On Sunday, to his disgust, he is confined to his box. The other horses in the yard may need a rest day but he would much prefer to be out taking more exercise.

By the middle of October 1977, Monksfield was ready for his warm-up runs on the flat. Michael Kinane was unavailable to ride him in the Irish Cesarewitch on the 15th so Des booked Paddy Sullivan, an experienced dark-haired jockey with a sad, mournful face. Paddy found himself right at the back of the large field, gave Monksfield a slap and a kick to wake him up and was then carried through the pack at an alarming rate before lack of

129

condition told. Four days later Des McDonogh wanted Dessie Hughes to ride Monksfield over hurdles in the Free Handicap at Punchestown, but the jockey had broken his left leg, just below the knee, at Kilbeggan during the summer and was not quite ready to resume. Tommy Kinane took his place and reported, after finishing sixth of eight, that the horse was still not fully wound up.

Only 10 days later a much fitter Monksfield finished third in the competitive 2-mile J. T. Rogers Memorial Gold Cup, ridden by Paddy Sullivan. Both trainer and jockey felt he was unlucky not to win. Des confirms, "He started his run a bit too late and finished like a train, but I was delighted to see him coming back to form so soon."

The second half of October was certainly a busy time for Monksfield. On October 31st, running for the fourth time in 17 days, ridden by Dessie Hughes on his return from injury, he was third to Meladon (receiving 24 pounds). Tommy Kinane partnered Lovely Bio, the second horse and no doubt annoyed at being replaced on Monksfield, set such a furious gallop that his old friend was unable to make an effective challenge. Says Tommy, "I was very upset about not riding Monksfield. I did my best to beat him and I did. Meladon only just caught me at the death and Monksfield was a long way back in third place."

It was still a highly satisfactory run under such a large weight and a mere six days later on November 5th the stage seemed set for his first victory of the season. Des McDonogh had found the perfect race for his star at Down Royal close to war-torn Belfast in Northern Ireland. He could not have wished for better conditions in the Name of the Game Trial Hurdle over two miles with only minor weight concessions to modest rivals on ideal going. But the early fireworks exploding to celebrate Guy Fawkes day in Northern Ireland were wholly absent from Monksfield's system that sombre day. Starting at 3/1 on to complete the formality of a clear round he ran deplorably. Lifeless from the start, he struggled home a distant third of seven to the old chaser Flashy Boy. Dessie Hughes, completely baffled, recalls, "That was the only occasion he was not a horse with me."

Des McDonogh could not understand what had happened.

130

The horse came home, ate his evening meal with his customary zeal and seemed perfectly all right the following morning. Anxious and puzzled Des spent as much time as possible with Monksfield but could not find a single clue to explain the uncharacteristically lifeless display at Down Royal. Helen was due to have their second child any day. Before she left for hospital they discussed the problem of Monksfield late into the night and decided to run him again at Leopardstown in a flat race on Saturday, November 12th, exactly a week after the disaster at Down Royal. "It might sound a strange thing to do," agrees Des McDonogh, "but his previous run was too bad to be true, we suspected something was wrong, and we wanted another opportunity to find out what it was."

As Joe Brady led Monksfield round the paddock at Leopardstown Des McDonogh, watching every movement intently, turned to a friend, Paddy Cussin, and said, "This horse is not right." He considered withdrawing him at that late stage but preferred to let the horse run so that he could have a second opinion from his young jockey Michael Kinane. Monksfield finished ninth of twenty-two runners to Mr Kildare, by no means a bad performance in such a high-class field, but Michael Kinane confirmed the trainer's fears as he reported, "This is not the same horse I've ridden before. He gave me no feel at all." Two years later Michael added, "Although he was quite definitely not right he still tried his heart out. He was running through beaten horses at the finish."

# 14

# 'I was sure
# he would die'

Monksfield spent the following day, Sunday, standing listlessly in his box. His appetite seemed the only healthy thing about him. Thoroughly alarmed Des McDonogh put a head collar on him and watched in dismay as one of his lads trotted the horse up and down the drive. "He was definitely yielding to his hind leg," he says.

Seamus Murphy, his regular vet, came to see the invalid on Monday morning. "By then," says Des, "he was obviously lame behind and was saving himself by walking on the point of his toe. The more he trotted round that morning the worse he looked." Twenty-four hours later a swelling appeared low down on Monksfield's off hind leg on the fetlock. Seamus Murphy prescribed a course of antibiotics but within days the swelling had spread with frightening speed up the leg around the pastern and cannon bone to engulf his hock. In the midst of Monksfield's illness Helen McDonogh gave birth to a second bouncing girl, Ashling. Each day she would look forward to her husband's visit and each time the sadness in his eyes told its own grim story. "I depressed her so much she asked me to stay away," he recalls.

Extensive and intensive treatment seemed to have no effect at all on Monksfield. The swelling on his hock grew as large as a grotesque balloon. "In that first week he just seemed to get worse every day," says Seamus Murphy. "Drugs did not work and I began to wonder if he would ever race again."

Des McDonogh would take turns with Joe Brady, Felix McCabe and other loyal supporters to bathe the crippled leg every three or four hours. Monksfield was so worn out, in constant pain, that he allowed his hind leg to be lifted and placed into a bucket of warm, soothing salt water. The next few days were the worst of Des McDonogh's life. "I never want to see again an animal disintegrate before my eyes to a skeleton," he says with feeling. "I was desperate. I knew in my mind he was finished. The flesh simply melted off him so swiftly I was sure we would lose him, that he would die."

The horse was lifeless, his eyes dull, his coat standing up straight; he could not move around the box and did not lie down for five weeks. Seamus Murphy's regular visits failed to lift the mood of gloomy despair. He recalls, "I was confident the horse would not die but he was fading away and in pain with it."

Late one evening Felix McCabe arrived to find the young trainer close to tears in Monksfield's box. "We both just stood there and I was so full up with it I could hardly speak to Felix," says Des. "There he was wasting away in front of our eyes and we could do nothing." Felix, too, was utterly dejected. He remembers, "As we bathed his leg that night I thought he was a write off. The muscles had all fallen off him and I could not sleep for thinking he was going to die."

Felix suggested a desperate solution. He knew a local sooth-sayer, a man reputed to have the power to heal a fatal disease of horses known as the Farcy. Des McDonogh realized that the man could not help but was prepared to clutch at the dimmest glimmer of hope. He admits, "I suppose I was in a mood to try anything." He giggles, "Mind you we made sure the man came in the middle of the night so that the vet would not be upset. Felix went off and brought this fellow to Monkey's box." The horse was so emaciated that he could feel every part of his hind leg. He touched and he probed and he eventually straightened his back and announced quietly it was not the Farcy.

Felix McCabe, deeply disappointed, croaked, "Are you sure it's not the Farcy?"

The crisis deepened. Antibiotics and other therapeutic drugs administered by injection all failed to halt Monksfield's deterioration. The next evening, fearing the horse was going to die, Des McDonogh rang Seamus Murphy to ask if a second vet could be brought in. Seamus, it transpired, was at Kells Golf

Club, so Des drove there and the vet, desperately anxious to cure his patient, readily agreed to a second opinion. They sat talking earnestly in Des McDonogh's car for three-quarters of an hour and decided to call in Bill Lyons, a well-known vet from Navan, who agreed at once to help.

Monksfield had already had some injections of folic acid. Now after taking a series of fresh blood tests, samples and X-rays Bill Lyons prescribed a course of folic acid, in tablet form, to be crushed into Monksfield's food.

Surprisingly Monksfield, the lionheart, is not a brave patient. Helen McDonogh confirms, "If he has the slightest thing wrong with him he pretends he is dying. He's a great baby, almost a coward over silly ailments." But now, under the best medical care, and with the whole village willing him to recover, he won the most important battle of his life.

Four days after Bill Lyons was called in Des McDonogh stepped dejectedly out of the bungalow to find Monksfield regarding him dolefully through the window of his box. He says, "I've never seen anything so marvellous in my life. There he was perking at the window. He had not been there for three weeks. You could see he was desperately tired but the light had come back into his eyes."

As soon as he had recovered sufficiently the vets suggested Monksfield should be led out for the briefest of walks. Joe Brady remembers, "At first he was too afraid to move. I could not do anything with him. Sometimes I would take him out to try to walk down to the end of the drive but he would stand still and refuse to take a step."

Progress at first was depressingly slow. Des McDonogh confirms, "He would not walk." After further consultation the vets decided he must be ridden to persuade him to move. The first time, ridden by his trainer, it took him twenty hesitant minutes to totter 100 yards to the end of the drive and back again. The skeleton of a wrecked lorry, abandoned years before, lay covered in weeds and grass on the side of the road a further hundred yards past the end of the drive. That unlikely landmark became a target for Monksfield's recovery. The day he walked there and back without pausing was cause for much celebration at Billywood.

134

He was still slightly lame, but walking a little sounder each day and the swelling was reducing all the time. The massive course of treatment finally cured the original infection but, says Seamus Murphy, it almost certainly affected his blood for he became seriously anaemic. Des McDonogh comments, "We have never discovered what caused the swelling. There was no injury there, not even a nick or a scratch to explain it. But after all the treatment his blood count dropped right down. So he needed more drugs for that."

Folic acid is a member of the Vitamin B group, commonly used in treatment of certain anaemias in man. It is found in green vegetable material, particularly spinach and also in yeast. Strangely enough, although it is readily absorbed when taken by mouth, it is not included in many of the familiar nutritional supplements fed to horses in training.

Michael Mangan, waiting anxiously for news on the other side of the Atlantic, took a particular interest in the cause of Monksfield's illness. Drawing on his extensive medical knowledge he developed a theory that lack of green grass in his horse's diet had led to anaemia. He explains, "The only source of folic acid is green grass. If you take a horse in from pasture at the end of July and put him into training he might spend nine months without eating any grass. So he becomes anaemic. Monksfield seems to be more prone to this in a much shorter space of time."

Dr Mangan continues, "Folic acid is necessary for the formation of red and white cells. White cells are the ones that fight infection. If you have a folic acid deficiency, not only are you anaemic, your red cells are not able to carry oxygen and your white cells are unable to fight infection. If a horse is deficient he cannot form red or white cells. Thus a prolonged course of folic acid was the correct treatment."

Monksfield's absence from the racecourse was noted by eagle-eyed pressmen, so Des issued a statement that he had an infection in his hind leg. He says, "I don't think anyone believed me. Rumours got back to me within days that he had tendon trouble, a leg injury, and would not race again."

The famous patient gradually regained strength as his daily walks increased in distance. The week before Christmas was a major milestone in his recuperation. He started trotting, but thoughts of racing and in particular Cheltenham, were still no more than absurdly ambitious dreams. Says Des McDonogh, "At that stage I had definitely ruled out Cheltenham and had told Michael Mangan so. He had been on the phone constantly and all along assured me the horse's welfare came first. The Champion Hurdle seemed an impossible target. Physically the horse had deteriorated so much, he'd lost all muscle and condition, his ribs showed, he was pot-bellied and he had melted away behind the saddle."

Exceptional horses confound even their closest admirers. Within a week of resuming trotting Monksfield was on his toes, kicking, jumping, a lively interested thoroughbred once more. The rapid rate of his progress astounded his young trainer. Des confirms, "Suddenly he started turning inside out. The transformation was complete. Gone was the sick and sorry invalid. He changed almost overnight into a full-blooded racehorse again. I never saw anything improve so swiftly. He was so full of himself that against my better nature I started to do steady canters on him."

Monksfield thrived on this gentle routine. He was working with so much zest that after careful consideration Des decided to run him at Navan on January 21st. He comments, "We were just hoping for a run that would tell us he was on the way back." Des tried to book Dessie Hughes but he was due to ride Chinrullah in the same race for Mick O'Toole. If Dessie Hughes had been available that day it's highly likely that Tommy Kinane would not have ridden Monksfield again, and much of the furore in March 1979 would have been avoided.

Des McDonogh explains, "Dessie was the man in possession, he was a top-class jockey, he got on well with the horse and we wanted him. But when we could not get him I put Tommy Kinane back on the horse thinking he knew Monksfield well enough to tell us if he was over the illness."

Chinrullah started favourite at 11/10 on but fell at the second hurdle. The next moment the unmistakably tubby figure of Monksfield pulled his way to the front going past the stands. He led briefly but faded in the last half-mile and coasted in one from last with Tommy Kinane motionless on his back. Tommy reports, "He was very big of himself that day and ran a super race

136

with all that weight. I held on to his head all the way and minded him. He showed no ill effects at all."

Des McDonogh was delighted. Only half-fit his horse had proved beyond any doubt that he had recovered all his old exuberant powers of aggression. Next morning Des took Monksfield for a quiet canter and found his old friend pulling his arms out with unexpected strength. He says, "I decided to try and prepare him for the Erin Foods race a month away even though I knew he could not possibly be ready in time. Cheltenham seemed a remote possibility still."

The weather was far from ideal for such a vital preparation. Snow and frost had caused meetings to be abandoned on both sides of the Irish Sea. The McDonoghs last success had been provided by the faithful Kavala at Powerstown Park in May and as they struggled out in the bitter mornings, frozen fingers barely able to grip reins, they began to wonder if they would ever win a race again. Monksfield alone raised their spirits. He had never worked so well at home. The fields at Billywood are scarcely large enough to cope with his fierce engine power at full song so Des began to take him to friends' farms where he could gallop further and more freely. Larry McGuinness owned an ideal field, almost 7 furlongs round. There Monksfield would complete three, sometimes four laps at a steady canter. He travelled to local racecourses too for serious gallops, and improved physically each day but just as his trainer had predicted the Erin Foods Hurdle on February 18th at Leopardstown came too soon.

Favourite for the race, at evens, was the English-trained Beacon Light, a brilliant horse on his day but an inconsistent one. Decent Fellow, another English hope, was joint second in the betting at 5/1 with the smart novice Mr Kildare. Monksfield, easy to back at 11/1, was always in the main group, disputed the lead at the last where he made a mistake and weakened in the final 100 yards to finish a close third to Prominent King and Mr Kildare.

Des and Helen McDonogh were overjoyed. He explains, "We thought if he stayed in touch to the second last hurdle then he was entitled to go to Cheltenham and did not dream he would rise at the last with a chance of winning. He was a little tired there

137

and made a mistake, though Tommy Kinane thought he would nearly have won if he had jumped it well."

Cheltenham was just over three weeks away. Monksfield now began to cover the most prodigious amount of miles in preparation for that supreme test and Larry McGuinness watched in awe as he lapped his field energetically with one, two and sometimes three other horses jumping in at various stages to keep him company. Tall, bespectacled, kind, a thoughtful man with a warm sense of humour, Larry McGuinness is the unnofficial chairman of Monksfield's vast fan club which is strongest in the small villages near Billywood. He recalls one particular training session in his field shortly before the 1978 Champion Hurdle. "Well," he declares, "you would not believe it if you were not there. 'Twas rather like a relay race only Monkey ran every leg against several different horses, beat them all off and afterwards he was so frisky, so full of himself, kicking and bucking and lashing out, with Des still on his back laughing like a mad thing."

# 15

# Champion

Des McDonogh decided that both Helen and Joe Brady should travel to Cheltenham for the 1978 Champion Hurdle, sponsored for the first time by Waterford Crystal. He reasoned that after all the problems of injury they might not have another chance to go there and so wanted them to share the enjoyment. Des flew over with Monksfield on Sunday; Helen and Joe followed on Tuesday.

Monksfield was in sparkling form as Des cantered him on Monday morning. Walking contentedly back to the stables they were overtaken by the familiar figure of Night Nurse who towered over his little rival. Des McDonogh called to his rider, "Make the most of this because it is the last time you will ever pass Monksfield."

Michael and Sheila Mangan jetted into England that day and headed for the Cotswolds with the usual team of supporters including Falah Maroun, George Battcock and Mick Maguire. Dinner that night with them was a little disquieting for Des McDonogh. He explains, "None of them would hear of defeat. If the horse had been on three legs or only two they would still have backed him. However much I repeated it they did not seem to realize how sick he had been before Christmas."

Monksfield's morning exercise on Tuesday was a revelation. He pulled furiously for a mile and a half, tugging his trainer's aching arms out of their sockets the whole way. "I could *barely* hold him," he confesses. "I knew he was fitter than he had ever been in his life. He had improved so much since his run in the Erin Foods." His glowing report at the breakfast table sent a

139

determined band of Monksfield's loyal supporters in search of the nearest betting shop still offering 10/1 against Monksfield's chance of winning the next day.

Des himself led the posse of five men. He is not a gambler in any sense of the word and his biggest bet until then had been an occasional £5 on the Tote. He had not backed Monksfield in any of his previous races but the morning's work–out had impressed him so deeply that he placed £100 on the counter in crisp notes and asked for £50 each way at 10/1. The girl assistant, perhaps more used to 10 pence doubles and trebles, looked surprised and said she would have to call head office. This took a few minutes and then she confirmed the bet. Mick Maguire next stepped up, placed rather more money on the counter and was forced to wait while another check call was put through to head office. The betting shop regulars, intrigued, watched the absurd charade repeated three more times as Monksfield's supporters including Falah Maroun helped themselves to a substantial slice of the 10/1 on offer. Des recalls, "There we were, all lined up like Brown's cows and she had to make separate phone calls for each of us. When we returned to the Queen's Hotel we told a few more friends about the price but they were offered only 8/1 at the shop." One of the men who settled for 8/1 was George Battcock, who, says Dr Mangan, thinks nothing of putting £500 on Monksfield each year in the Champion Hurdle. He insists, "Some of my friends now think backing Monksfield at Cheltenham is just as simple as putting their money into a machine, pulling a lever and doubling or trebling it."

Certainly on Tuesday night defeat was not considered at their annual pre-race dinner at Don Pasquale's Italian restaurant in Gloucester. Their confidence had been boosted by the knowledge that neither Night Nurse nor Sea Pigeon, Monksfield's two most obvious rivals, would be ridden by their regular jockeys.

Poor Paddy Broderick had suffered severe head injuries, that caused his eventual retirement, when Night Nurse fell at Kempton on Boxing Day and had not ridden since. This left Peter Easterby's jockey, the brilliant Jonjo O'Neill, soon to be a record-breaking champion, juggling with the delicate task of deciding between his old friend Sea Pigeon and the dual champion hurdler, Night Nurse, an agonizing choice which he solved by staying with Sea Pigeon. Colin Tinkler, an experienced Northern jockey, was booked for Night Nurse, but an eventful day's racing on Tuesday soon changed those plans, for both men were injured.

Severely concussed when Grangewood Girl fell in the 2 mile Champion Chase, Jonjo, under a sensible new safety rule, was unable to ride in a race for the next seven days. Late in the afternoon he had recovered sufficiently to join in a conference with Pat Muldoon and Peter Easterby to pick his replacement. Their first choice, Tommy Carberry, was due to ride Meladon in the Champion Hurdle and could not be released. Frank Berry, however, was available and was quickly snapped up. Sea Pigeon is looked after at home by Mark Birch who flirted briefly with a career as a hairdresser before becoming a polished flat race jockey. Mark was at Cheltenham to see his favourite horse run and together with Jonjo O'Neill was able to pass on some useful hints about Sea Pigeon to Frank Berry.

Colin Tinkler feared he had broken some bones in his foot when Samuel Pepys crashed at the third last fence in the Novice Chase. The foot blew up so quickly that John Suthern, who had also fallen at the same fence, just pulled off Colin's boot in time. The top of his foot ballooned to the size and texture of an angry black tennis ball and so the former champion jockey Ron Barry was provisionally engaged to ride Night Nurse.

Colin Tinkler took enough pain-killers to knock him out for the night and woke to find the swelling had subsided considerably, spent the morning bathing his foot alternately in hot and cold water, smothered it with cream and limped purposefully to the racecourse to announce he was fit to ride.

Tommy Kinane, meanwhile, had other worries on his mind. His wife Frances was seriously ill in bed at home with a heart condition. Tommy stayed for Cheltenham, as usual, with relatives at Hayes on the western outskirts of London and was driven to the course in the morning with his two nephews. They arrived shortly before midday and set out to walk the course, the small, chunky, jutting-jawed figure of Tommy Kinane completely dwarfed by his two young nephews. In confident mood Tommy started to run. He recalls, "I was feeling so fit that I even jumped some of the hurdles but my two nephews, hardy fellows both of them, could not live with me. I *sprinted* down the hill to the last hurdle but did not jump it because there were too many people around it."

The first race of Champion Hurdle day, 1978, will long be remembered for Golden Cygnet's runaway victory in the Waterford Crystal Supreme Novices' Hurdle. Unbeaten in four previous races, he was backed down to 4/5 as if defeat was out of the question, pulled his way to the front at the second last flight with his jockey sitting motionless and sprinted up the hill to beat Western Rose by an astounding 15 lengths with a competitive field that included thirteen individual winners stretched far behind. John Burke, rider of the runner-up, commented, "Western Rose would not have won even if he had been on high octane fuel. We think the world of Western Rose so Golden Cygnet must be a machine to beat him so comprehensively."

It was a hugely impressive display and one generous ante-post bookmaker who recklessly offered 10/1 against Golden Cygnet for the next year's Champion Hurdle was instantly swamped by punters in a stampede of gold rush proportions. While those eager gamblers speculated on a race 12 months hence the field for the 1978 Waterford Crystal Champion Hurdle was already parading with Night Nurse, the 3/1 favourite to win record prize money for the race of £21,332; more, curiously, than the great Sir Ken won throughout his entire hurdling career. Bracketed together at 5/1 were Sea Pigeon and the previous year's disappointing favourite Birds Nest, bidding to become the first blinkered horse to win the race for some 30 years. Monksfield was just about the best-backed horse in the last fifteen hectic minutes of activity in the ring. Certainly there was not a sign of the 10/1 on offer only the previous morning. A miserly 6/1 was the best price to be found and constant support at that figure caused the bookies to cut his odds half a point to 11/2. He looked outstanding in the paddock, too, on his toes, jig-jogging proudly, led round by Joe Brady who was sporting a smart new knitted woollen orange hat, one of several handed out earlier in the day to Monksfield's clan by Falah Maroun.

Huddled together in the paddock Des McDonogh and Tommy Kinane agreed that Monksfield should track Night

Nurse, keep in touch with him going down the hill and take the lead soon enough to test the suspect stamina of Sea Pigeon who was likely to be held up again for his customary later burst. Michael Mangan confirms, "Night Nurse worried us most. I thought he was the most superb hurdler I had ever seen."

Nearby in the paddock Colin Tinkler, who had ridden without discomfort in the first race, stood, legs crossed, wearing an odd pair of boots, the left one a size or two larger than the right. He recalls, "We were hoping that the erratic Levaramoss would go off in front at his usual 100 m.p.h. so that he could tow me along at least to half-way." Frank Berry, in the same group, was advised to ride a patient waiting race on Sea Pigeon.

As Monksfield left the paddock to parade with his twelve opponents in front of the stands, his breeder Peter Ryan ran into Michael Mangan. Ryan's interest in racing had remained strictly limited but he had followed the career of the little colt he had bred in such unusual circumstances and in January 1978, during a rush of blood to the head, had put £10 each way on him at 12/1, the best available odds for the Champion Hurdle at the time. On the big day Peter Ryan, with three friends, travelled to Cheltenham on the race train, lunching on overcooked roast beef, washed down with the very best vino that British Rail could muster. Michael Mangan gave him a warm reception, the two men arranged to meet later and Peter walked down to the last flight of hurdles for a close-up view of the race.

Back at Inch in Ireland where Monksfield had been reared, Peter's cousin Arthur Ryan was ill with yet another bout of flu but he pottered downstairs from his sick bed to watch the race on television. A few miles away in Tipperary Frances Kinane, against doctors orders, struggled out of bed to watch her husband on television. She admits, "It was a foolish thing to do but it was a rare chance to see Tommy riding in England and I did not want to miss it. I was much too excited which was bad for my heart." At school her son Jayo's eager request to watch the race was turned down by his unsympathetic teacher. Jayo's eldest brother Thomas had no such problem. Already an amateur jockey he was at Cheltenham to ride in a race the following day.

At the start Roger Rowell faced an anxious few minutes on the

143

tearaway outsider Levaramoss, one of three colts in the race. A frantically hard puller, Levaramoss was a useful front runner on his day but had developed a habit of downing tools at the start as often as a militant docker. Despite a change of trainer he had refused to start in his previous two races but, before that, had beaten the much improved Kybo at Fontwell.

Levaramoss was in a particularly unco-operative mood on March 15th 1978, and stood defiantly flat footed as Night Nurse led the rest of the field at a steady pace towards the first flight of hurdles. Des McDonogh, watching from his usual perch high up in the stands, noted with pleasure that Tommy Kinane was immediately able to take up an ideal position a length or so behind the leader on the inside rail. By the time the recalcitrant Levaramoss consented to jump off, the field had streamed past the stands and was heading out into the country towards the third hurdle. Down that back stretch Night Nurse continued to lead with Monksfield harrying constantly on the inside.

Colin Tinkler recalls, "I knew I wouldn't win even at half-way when Tommy Kinane tried to squeeze up my inner. His horse was going so easily while I was already 'niggle niggle' on Night Nurse."

Tommy Kinane, in marked contrast, was bubbling with confidence. He says, "My plan was to push and bustle the leader along. I wanted to torment him the whole way. I even gave Night Nurse a couple of kicks with my foot in the backside as we started up the hill."

Tommy Kinane's cheeky attempt to poke up Night Nurse's inside after jumping the fifth hurdle earned instant retribution. As the hurdle course passed close to the wing of a fence on the adjacent steeplechase track Colin Tinkler moved slightly left handed to close the gap. The video film of the race confirms his comment, "I just edged across him there to keep him in place." Tommy Kinane had to pull back rather sharply but the manoeuvre cost him little ground and soon after jumping the sixth hurdle at the highest point of the course Monksfield's handsome head showed in front, briefly, for the first time.

Sweeping left handed at the top bend Monksfield and Night Nurse matched strides as they ran down to the third last hurdle. Behind them Kybo was already beginning to weaken and Birds

144

Nest was quite unable to get in a blow, but Dramatist and Master Monday were still well placed and Sea Pigeon was moving through from the rear with ominous ease.

Tommy Kinane now made the decisive move of the race. He recalls, "I was thinking, Jeez, it's time to get out of here or those fellows behind will be coming with a run. I knew he would stay up that final hill so I set sail for home, away with me, and catch me if you can. We flew down the hill, soared over the second last, and were clear on the rail so tight the fleas could not have got up my inside." To his eternal credit Tommy Kinane did not look behind him. If he had done so he would have seen the familiar tartan colours of Sea Pigeon still closing and Master Monday, too, moving easily on his quarters. Master Monday's challenge collapsed in five brief strides on the bend and as Monksfield headed for the last hurdle Frank Berry produced Sea Pigeon to tackle him on the stands side.

Fifty yards from the final hurdle they were almost level. Watching from his pitch beside the jump Peter Ryan felt an instant yet unexpected tremor of excitement surge through his body. Here, a year ago, Monksfield had thrown away a winning chance with a rare blunder. This time he met the hurdle perfectly, threw his heart out far to the other side, gained a precious length and landed with the race already won. Tommy Kinane admits, "I saw a long stride. I really rode him for it and he stood off a long way. Sea Pigeon was there on my shoulder but at the speed we were travelling I knew Frank could not be sitting too cushy."

Far from that, Frank Berry was distinctly uneasy on the final approach to the last hurdle. He says, "Four strides away I knew I was beaten unless Monksfield made a mistake. My horse had given me as much as he could for coaxing and pushing so I went for my stick as a last resort." Sea Pigeon responded gamely enough but could not quicken up the steep hill and as stamina increasingly came into play, Monksfield strode away majestically for the line.

Tommy Kinane remembers, "I knew I had burned out Sea Pigeon but even so I wanted to be sure so I picked up my whip and gave my fellow just one crack and drove to the winning post without ever touching him again."

A bold leap by Monksfield ensures his victory in the 1978
Waterford Crystal Champion Hurdle. Sea Pigeon is
crossing the hurdle. *Credit: George Selwyn*

Down at the last hurdle Peter Ryan realized Monksfield was
going to win. He laughs, "Everyone was jumping and shouting
as the two horses came past and I found to my extreme surprise
that I was doing the same thing. It was certainly one of the most
exciting moments of my life ... comparable to watching a
Saturn rocket, live at Cape Canaveral, taking off for the Moon. It
was a hugely emotional moment to see this small horse that I had
bred running up the steep hill to a wildly enthusiastic reception. I
don't think I could have been more pleased if I had owned him."

In the final 150 yards Monksfield began to edge left as he
fought his way up the hill, his beautiful head thrust out low in the
most determined style. At the line he was two lengths ahead
with the brave former champion Night Nurse a long looking six
lengths back in third place.

In that inspiring moment of triumph as the huge crowd

honoured a new champion, his young trainer, overcome with emotion, sank to his knees to offer a prayer of thanks. Seconds later he was lifted from the ground by a friend, Willie Brown, who feared he had collapsed. Des was just 31 years and 11 months old, exactly the same age as Vincent O'Brien when he won his first Champion Hurdle with Hatton's Grace in 1949. Des recalls, "I knew Monkey had it won at the last. A tired horse does not stand off to jump where he did. Helen was shouting hysterically and we were both mad with joy." Only later did he realize it was the first winner he had trained for 10 months.

Somehow Des and Helen battled through the cheering crowd towards the winner's enclosure where thousands of Irishmen were already waiting to applaud their first winner of the Champion Hurdle since Winning Fair in 1963. Peter Ryan skirted around the chaos and met Michael Mangan, choking back the emotion, and his wife Sheila who was in danger of being carried away in the enthusiasm of the moment. The Mangans eventually reached the side of the weighing room as renewed cheers welcomed the sight of Monksfield, jinking jauntily, led by Joe

Monksfield strides away up the final hill as Sea Pigeon lands over the last hurdle.    *Credit: George Selwyn*

Monksfield and Tommy Kinane return to a wildly
enthusiastic reception, led in by the winning owner
Michael Mangan. Note the emotion on his face.

*Credit: George Selwyn*

Brady in his orange hat. Michael Mangan grasped Monksfield's
bridle, gave him a warm pat of thanks, then led him proudly
down the narrow slope into the hallowed winner's circle amid a
crescendo of cheers. Behind them Peter Ryan put his arm round
Sheila Mangan and together they were swept through the tiny
funnel into the multitude of boisterous supporters. Minutes later
Des and Helen McDonogh finally fought their way through, to
fresh applause, and Peter Easterby, trainer of the second and
third, walked over to say a quiet 'well done'. Pat Muldoon, too,
was one of the first to offer his congratulations.

Someone in the milling throng asked Peter Ryan if he re-
gretted selling Monksfield. Laughing happily he shook his head.
There are many strange chance events in the history of
Monksfield and Peter Ryan knew better than anyone the remote

possibility of such a perfect victory by the horse he bred in his own colours under the supervision of another, more conventional trainer.

He says, "Standing in the winner's enclosure I was aware of Monksfield being a special kind of hero; that he was not a Turf Club horse; that he came from another world to that of the red-faced generals sipping small quantities of champagne with the successful team. There was this tall surgeon from Newfoundland, the bright eyed trainer – a man of incredible dedication and force – the sturdy, wry jockey and all those men from across the water fattening their rolls of folding money as the bookies paid out. And for a moment or two I savoured being part of the happy ending of an unlikely but true story."

At Inch Arthur Ryan, elated at the success of the horse he had been instrumental in breeding, opened his drink cupboard to reach for the bottle of champagne he had earned for winning his last point-to-point four years previously. When he finally padded back up the stairs to bed much, much later that evening there was a fresh spring in his step. Recovery had begun in the best possible way.

Arthur Ryan's jubilation may in part have been increased by the knowledge that Monksfield's success that afternoon had added a hundred pounds or so to the family coffers, thanks to the ISIS scheme which encouraged breeders and rewarded them for success. The money was credited each time to Peter Ryan but he was anxious his cousin should have an equal share of this bonus. Arthur Ryan watched in amusement as Tommy Kinane was produced for an impromptu interview with Julian Wilson on BBC television. On some occasions his interviews can be a little too heavy for the casual viewer but this time his subject was not in the mood for serious discussion. The next five minutes proved to be an uproariously funny advertisement for the Kinane clan.

"Just how big is your family?" asked Wilson. Tommy turned to point to a huge tented village below them and laughed, "If you got all the Kinanes together they would not fit into that mass of tents." Later he added in reply to another question, "I'm far too young to think of retiring but I have three sons already riding and I suppose I ought to think about giving them a chance." Afterwards Tommy reported eagerly, "People were telling me I

149

150 A superb shot of Monksfield and Des McDonogh in the
winner's circle. *Credit: George Selwyn*

interviewed Julian rather than the other way round."

A few yards away Frank Berry was holding a dejected post mortem with Pat Muldoon and Peter Easterby. Frank recounted, "Monksfield stretched me coming down the hill but round the elbow on the final bend I was just timing my run so that I would land in front over the last hurdle. All the way to the last I was closing and still thinking I would win until I picked up my whip. Sea Pigeon kept on but the other horse just stayed better than mine up the hill and *wore* him down." Frank thought Sea Pigeon was good enough to have won a Champion Hurdle in an ordinary year and added that he was very unlucky to have met such a tough horse as Monksfield.

Back in the weighing room Tommy was handed a telegram from a certain Paddy Broderick saying, "Congratulations, sorry I could not be with you at the last." Tommy immediately sent out £100 for a case of champagne. Calling over Jeff King and Andy Turnell he told them, "Now, boys, I'm off to London, so please see that everyone gets a drink. Give me two bottles to take with me and I'll be gone." He explains, "Dr Mangan invited me to the celebration dinner but I thought I would ride another winner the next day and did not want a late night whatever the excuse." So Tommy Kinane, the ageing hero of the day, was driven back to Hayes and took his relatives out for a quiet meal.

Peter Ryan, too, returned to London, on the packed race special, then moved quickly on to Finch's where the waiting landlord Patrick McEvoy led them upstairs to watch the re-run of the race on the BBC's 'Sportsnight' programme. Naturally Patrick had laid on an immense amount of champagne and Peter does not remember at all clearly how he reached home in the small hours of the morning.

Down at the racecourse stables the hero of the day was jumping and kicking as though he had not had any exercise. The horse was so full of himself that Joe Brady found it difficult to wash him down before taking him to the veterinary box for the dope test automatically carried out on big race winners. Monksfield jogged friskily into the spacious box, then to the surprise of the vets and their assistants immediately knelt down on the thickly laid straw and performed his customary victory roll. The dope test over, he returned to his own box where he rolled happily on

Tommy Kinane, Des McDonogh and Michael Mangan
caught in jubilant mood after the presentations.
*Credit: Sporting Pictures*

his back once more. The victorious owner and trainer arrived with their wives to find him tucking into his evening feed with accustomed gusto.

Later the jubilant group was cheered loudly as they entered the Queen's Hotel. Michael Mangan with typical generosity organized a victory banquet at the Queen's that night and unlike so many owners did not forget to invite the lad Joe Brady, who had led up Monksfield that day. The feast for some forty carousers was in full swing when the message came through that the magnificent Champion Hurdle Trophy, freshly inscribed, had been delivered at the hotel reception desk. Des McDonogh slipped out to collect it and as he walked back through the packed dining-room, proudly holding the famous trophy, all conversation ceased to be replaced by a thunderous ovation of clapping and cheering. The trophy, filled repeatedly with champagne, was passed round for everyone to taste. Even Des McDonogh felt sufficiently carried away by the moment to risk his teetotal reputation as he sipped a mouthful of the bubbly. "It was *horrible*," he recalls, "I just hate the smell of it."

Every so often he would reach out to touch the Champion Hurdle Cup. Soon the speeches began. There was a warm motion of thanks by Michael Mangan to all those, especially Des and Helen McDonogh and Tommy Kinane, who had helped Monksfield achieve such a famous triumph. Mick Maguire spoke, so too did George Battcock and Jack Kelsey. Des McDonogh, too, tried to speak but his normally reliable vocal chords had succumbed to the punishment of his wild cheering earlier. Poems were recited and soon the singing began. The party finally broke up in the early hours of the morning. Des McDonogh remembers, "I couldn't sleep very well that night because I was so elated. I felt as though I was on a cloud two feet above the mattress."

# 16

# 'The Bookies were blistered with him'

The revellers stumbled out of bed the next morning, rubbing their eyes in disbelief at the sight of huge snowflakes swirling down on the white-coated Gloucestershire countryside. Already a blanket of snow lay several inches thick in Cheltenham and Thursday's card, including the Piper Champagne Gold Cup, had to be postponed for a month. Early in the morning Des McDonogh popped round to the betting shop to collect his winnings. The manager, white faced, his eyes downcast, admitted, "We've just enough cash to pay you but all your friends will have to wait until we can go to the bank." His pockets bulging, Des moved on to meet Joe Brady at the racecourse stables. Monksfield looked well enough but his trainer did not wish to subject him to a hard journey in such foul conditions and so decided to give him an extra twenty-four hours rest before sending him home. Back at the hotel George Battcock was preparing to collect his substantial winnings in a bag before taking his wife off for a skiing holiday in Switzerland. Des and Helen meanwhile headed for Birmingham airport and a delay of many hours before their plane took off for Dublin.

Unknown to them extravagant plans were being laid to welcome Monksfield home. Larry McGuinness, Felix McCabe and Pat Cussin, thinking the horse was expected back early on Thursday evening, rounded up hundreds of admirers and well wishers. Larry points out, "You realize what Monkey and Des have done between them. There are an awful lot of fellows round this part of the country who never had a bet before he came along and are now compulsive gamblers. Dozens of local

154

people travelled over to England to see him win and thousands round here backed him. Locally he's far more popular than Arkle and the bookies took a terrible hammering. They were blistered with him," he adds with obvious relish.

Larry McGuinness and his friends organized a cavalcade of some three hundred cars to greet the horse-box carrying Monksfield on the homeward journey; horns tooting, lights flashing, they stretched for four miles on the road from Kells towards Navan. The town band was quickly assembled to play the returning hero home through Kells, on to Moynalty, round by Mullagh and finally back to Billywood. Everything was ready for a triumphant procession but the star of the show failed to appear. The welcoming committee did not know of Des McDonogh's decision to send Monksfield home 24 hours late. Even so the combination of lengthy flight delays and bad weather would have caused him to miss his adoring fans. Shortly before 1 a.m. on Friday the taxi carrying Des and Helen McDonogh, slumped fast asleep in the back seat, passed the few remaining cars waiting forlornly for Monksfield.

Michael Mangan, continuing his holiday, came to Ireland, too, and threw a big party for the McDonoghs, their friends and all the lads from the stable at the Beechmount Hotel in Navan. There were more speeches and this time Des McDonogh, his voice fully recovered, was able both to speak and sing. Michael Mangan, too, sang, as did Des' mother and the promising young apprentice jockey Frank Skelly. A week later, on Saturday, March 25th, Michael Mangan held another dinner, this time in Cashel, for Tommy Kinane and his family and friends.

Dozens of telegrams and letters of congratulations reached Billywood, many of them addressed direct to Monksfield. An owner, Terry Mooney, wrote, "We were practically in tears watching Monksfield storm up the hill at Cheltenham for a moment of unforgettable glory," adding somewhat ambiguously, "I have never seen my wife so excited in my life."

Another admirer wrote, "Monksfield gave me the thrill of a lifetime. I know now what Red Rum's followers felt when he won the Grand National for a third time last year."

A letter came from the secretary of Des' old Rugby Club in Limerick saying, "Those who played with you in your Old

155

Crescent days are now revelling in your reflected glory. You certainly did not spare yourself when you played for us and Monksfield appears to have inherited some of your grit. He puts down his head and takes them on.''

Several requests were made for Monksfield's racing plates, and in one case, for Dr Mangan's silks. There was even a note from a friendly bank manager in Galway. Des McDonogh's Aunt Eileen, a nun, wrote from England, "What a wonderful win; *poor* Night Nurse must be very disappointed. I shook hands with you on television yesterday as you put the rugs back on Monksfield. He is a wonderful little horse and a number of the sisters put a few shillings on him.''

The object of all this adulation, in spectacular form at home, was ready to return to England for a repeat duel with Night Nurse in the Templegate Hurdle. Des McDonogh reports, "Each year he seems to improve after Cheltenham. He's certainly at his best in the spring with the sun on his back. After his Champion Hurdle victory you could almost see him improve a little each day. I just could not believe this was the same horse that had been at death's door four months earlier.''

Monksfield's jockey, however, was not at all well. Tommy Kinane, perhaps a little unwisely, did not adopt Paddy Broderick's sensible policy of riding only over hurdles. A very fit man, he felt perfectly justified in continuing to ride some good and bad steeplechasers in his chosen role as a freelance jockey. He had fallen on Kintai at Leopardstown on the day of the Erin Foods Hurdle, and now, just five days before Liverpool in the Irish Distillers' Grand National he suffered a pile-driving fall on his head on the same horse, which left him rolling in agony on the ground, gasping for breath. Tommy Kinane, as we have discovered, is an extremely tough character. Despite the most agonizing pain in his back he eventually limped back to the weighing room and told the waiting doctor, quite untruthfully, that he felt all right. He dressed in extreme pain, found someone to drive him home, picked at a meal and only then agreed to be taken to the local hospital at Cashel. There he was found to have broken three vertebrae, two in his back and one in his neck, and to have damaged both lungs. He spent the next fortnight flat on his back unable to move. Later he was allowed home on the strict

156

condition that he promised to stay in bed for another month.

So Dessie Hughes was back on Monksfield again at Liverpool. Des McDonogh travelled the horse over while Helen and Joe Brady arrived later in the week. The night before the race Des and some friends, including Barney Reilly, the best man at his wedding, were turned away at the door of a casino in Liverpool run by Ladbrokes. They were about to leave when Barney called to the doorman, "You may not want him now," pointing at Des, "but you'll be looking for him this time tomorrow when he has won a big race at your meeting at Aintree."

A minute later they were ushered inside where Des met Pat Muldoon, the cheerful, silvery-haired Scots owner of Sea Pigeon. The two men spent a contented evening discussing their favourite topics and when Muldoon left he offered Des a lift to his hotel. Also in the car was another friend of Muldoon's, John Watt, tall and dark, who had spent the day searching in vain for Des McDonogh to tell him the good news that he had been voted Pommery and Greno trainer of the month of March by a panel of racing journalists. John was finally able to arrange for the presentation of the case of Pommery, plus a Salmanazer (holding the equivalent of twelve bottles) to be made after the Templegate Hurdle.

This time Monksfield, as the reigning champion, was set to give 5 pounds to his old rival Night Nurse, now ridden by Jonjo O'Neill. The difference in weights no doubt accounted for the surprising fact that Night Nurse, at 13/8, was preferred in the betting market to Monksfield, who was allowed to start at the generous price of 9/4, with the novice Mr Kildare, an impressive Cheltenham winner, strongly supported at 3/1. Once again Monksfield proved the bookmakers wrong. Night Nurse led from the start, and behind him, Dessie Hughes, to his delight, found Monksfield moving with unaccustomed ease. Dessie recalls, "The year before Monksfield had been such a *tough* ride but this time we turned into the home straight beside Night Nurse, cantering, *absolutely cantering*," his voice rises sharply in surprise. "I went up and joined Jonjo on the final bend and my horse was cruising so easily I could not believe we did not have to go round again." Monksfield drew steadily clear, jumped the last in front and held Night Nurse's renewed challenge by two

Smiling in the rain. Des
McDonogh after
receiving his award as
Pommery Trainer of the
Month for March, 1978.

lengths with Kybo fully 10 lengths back in third place.

Dessie Hughes was taken to hospital less than an hour later after his Grand National mount, the outsider War Bonnet, nose-dived at the third fence firing him heavily into the ground. He coughed up blood in hospital for a few days, pronounced himself fit, and returned home to Ireland.

Over-zealous customs officials in Dublin confiscated the Pommery champagne, took $2\frac{1}{2}$ hours to search the horse-box and held on to the precious liquid for six weeks. When the 'bubbly' finally reached Billywood two bottles were missing.

Monksfield enjoyed a brief rest after Liverpool before his annual outing on the flat in the Halverstown Apprentice Plate at Naas. Ridden as usual by Michael Kinane he started an odds-on favourite and won easily to complete his hat-trick in the event.

The very same afternoon at Ayr Golden Cygnet's meteoric career came to a tragic end when he fell heavily in the lead at the final flight of the Scottish Champion Hurdle, injured vertebrae in his neck and died 48 hours later. In his brief, glittering racing life he had shown all the qualities of a champion, above all the exhilarating and essential ability to spring away from his rivals in just a few seconds. Ironically his fatal injury occurred at the very moment he was poised to beat the finest hurdlers in Britain, including Sea Pigeon and Night Nurse.

So the much trumpeted encounter between Monksfield and Golden Cygnet did not take place. His trainer, Edward O'Grady, desolate at his horse's untimely death, is convinced Golden Cygnet was good enough to have won the 1978 Champion Hurdle while still a novice. Des McDonogh, you will not be surprised to hear, disagrees. He says, "I was desperately sorry when Golden Cygnet was killed but ever since it happened everyone has been telling me he would have beaten Monksfield when they met. The form book does not suggest that is right; experience counts for at least 10 lengths and I've yet to see a horse that can outjump or outstay Monksfield."

Four days after winning his third successive Halverstown Apprentice Plate Monksfield met much stiffer opposition in the £3,000 Savel Beg Stakes at Leopardstown, ridden, unusually on the flat, by Dessie Hughes who was just able to do the correct weight of 9 stone, 13 pounds. The field of twenty-two included several useful long-distance horses yet Monksfield, starting joint 3/1 favourite with Midland Gayle, outstayed them all to beat Rathinree, who he met at level weights, by 1½ lengths. It was the first time Monksfield had won on the track and Dessie Hughes' first winner on the flat for ten years. He remembers, "They did him for speed early on; he was off his feet and could not go with them. But his courage saw him through that day and he stayed on powerfully at the end."

Des McDonogh insists, "He won with his ears pricked and was on the crest of a wave." Des had entered Monksfield in the new, richly sponsored Royal Doulton Handicap Hurdle at Haydock on May 1st. He reasons, "I thought the horse had never been better and it would have been a shame to have stayed at home and seen a lesser animal win the race."

Larry McGuinness and his friends had quietly organized a dinner dance for the McDonoghs at the Beechmount Hotel four days before Haydock. Four hundred and fifty tickets were snapped up within days and hundreds more applicants were disappointed. Guest speakers included Michael O'Hehir, a deservedly popular man whose distinctive tones as a commentator have made him a household name in racing circles on both sides of the Atlantic. Films of the Champion Hurdle and Templegate Hurdle were shown to rapturous applause. Michael Mangan, asked to send a telegram of congratulation to the dinner, replied, "I can do better than that", and flew over from Newfoundland just for the function at which an inscribed silver tray was presented to his trainer.

Monksfield's trip to Haydock took a tiring 20 hours. The horse-box lost its way at one stage, and when the boat finally docked in England there was a further 4-hour delay at customs. The ground, too, was much firmer than the new champion liked and the flat hurdles course, with two sharp bends, was certainly not ideal for his enormous reserves of stamina. Monksfield and Sea Pigeon, joint top weights with 12 stone, were set to give Night Nurse 5 pounds, with half the field on the bottom 10-stone mark. On the strength of his recent victory over Night Nurse in the Scottish Champion Hurdle Sea Pigeon was installed favourite at 5/2 with Monksfield second in the betting at 100/30, and Night Nurse at 8/1.

Night Nurse raced away at such a furious gallop that his two chief opponents were quite unable to stay near him. Turning for home Sea Pigeon was already beaten and Monksfield, too, struggling half-way down the field, appeared to face a quite impossible task. Dessie Hughes recalls, "It was *pure endurance* that got him into the picture. We had been going flat out the whole way and the only time I got a bit of heart was when he threw a fantastic leap at the third last and passed at least four horses in the air." Two more superlative jumps helped shrink the gap further and as Monksfield touched down over the last hurdle it seemed for one moment that he might catch the new leader Royal Gaye, one of the bottom weights. He tried, *how* he strained to reach the horse in front of him, closing the gap with every stride, but the concession of 2 stone proved too severe a burden and he finished second, beaten just three-quarters of a length, with Night Nurse 2½ lengths away third and Sea Pigeon a long way behind in eighth place. A mere nine days later Sea

160

Pigeon won the Chester Cup under top weight!

Such a gallant defeat, if anything, added to Monksfield's reputation as the bravest horse in training. He would not give in
when faced with an overwhelming task, and was cheered as
loudly as the winner on his return to the unsaddling enclosure.
Royal Gaye set a new track record that day but the terrible strain
of defeating the champion may have broken his heart because the
following season he was but a shadow of his former self.

# 17

# The Steam Thrashing Festival

By the summer of 1978 Billywood had developed into a flourishing racing stable with more new boxes and some twenty-five horses in training. Another lad had joined the team but the system remained much as before with the McDonoghs and their helpers each mucking out six boxes before the major task of riding out all the horses in lots of three and four. Des McDonogh was surprised rather than bitter that his achievements with Monksfield had not reaped the expected harvest of more promising young horses to train. He is used to the disappointment now and accepts that unlike many successful trainers, he is not prepared to spend time socializing in clubs, hotels and other spots where potential owners might be found. He prefers to stay at home, spending his time learning the idiosyncrasies of his horses, even though the majority of them tend to be distinctly moderate.

He comments, "A lot of people in this country still think it has been a fluke the whole way with Monksfield. We are happy to remain unfashionable, but three-quarters of our horses are not very good and I feel that we deserve, well, a little better. Helen and I are very much a team; I know I would never have made a trainer on my own. She's a tremendous worker and judge, and we discuss everything we are going to do with the horses. She's the grafter, *thrives* on hard work and the place would just not go without her. On the *coldest* day in the winter she will be straight out into the yard, cleaning out six boxes or more before waking the two girls for breakfast. I suppose if we had half as many horses and better quality, we would all be better off but I'm not cribbing at all, it's just great to have a hand in the game."

The particular day Des McDonogh was talking had been a long, painful and arduous one. He had been knocked out for a few minutes in the morning in a rare fall and had spent a difficult and uncomfortable afternoon at the races. Now late in the evening he insisted on walking round the yard in the warm summer air, topping up many of the horses' water buckets.

Pausing at the water trough as he filled two more buckets Des McDonogh shrugged resignedly as he delivered the most unlikely verdict on his own methods. "I am", he said quite seriously, "more of an *old slogger*, really, than a trainer. Several trainers have told me I don't give a good image of myself by spending so much time working in the yard alongside the lads. But it is the way Helen and I prefer."

How, I wondered, would Monksfield have fared in a larger, more conventional racing stable? He paused for a moment, then shook his head. "If he had been with a Curragh trainer he would probably have been put in the second, overflow yard. I just can't *imagine* Monksfield with eighty or one hundred other horses around him; I'm sure he would have been bored by the monotony of the routine, totally lost. You see he never shows anything in his work at home so I expect after a couple of races on the flat as a 3-year-old he would have been gelded. If that had happened . . . well I suppose he would have slipped into obscurity."

Early in the summer of 1978 a huge, yellow Mercedes bearing a Northern Ireland number plate purred up the short drive at Billywood. The three occupants showed no sign whatsoever of stepping out of the car so Des, intrigued, climbed into the back seat to talk to them. They wanted to know if he had room for a horse, Stranfield, a 5-year-old who had won one race and was ready to go back into training. Choking back the immediate thought that he had room for ten horses, Des agreed to take Stranfield and arranged for him to arrive the following day.

Stranfield and Des McDonogh did not like each other from the very start; both are independent, at times awkward characters. Des admits, "We agreed to disagree, I suppose we are two narky people together." Lawrence McGuinness, son of Larry, had recently joined the yard to learn the racing game. A placid young man, carrot thatched, hungry for knowledge, Lawrence was keen to look after the new addition. It was a perfect match. A horse with a scintillating late burst of speed, Stranfield clearly thrived on the personal attention of his new lad and the gentle handling in his race by the stable apprentice Frank Skelly, who was under strict instructions not to use the whip. Ridden by Frank, Stranfield finished a close fourth on his first run for his new stable and then proceeded to win four competitive handicaps in 6 weeks and added a fifth victory in another handicap at Leopardstown towards the end of the season.

The stable prospered in the summer of 1978. On a golden Saturday in June at Phoenix Park, Lisahunny and Dervor, both 2-year-olds and ridden by Frank Skelly, recorded Des McDonogh's first double as a trainer. Dr Michael Mangan's third racehorse Gatelle, another cheap purchase, finally won a maiden hurdle at Naas, and the Pommery champagne, when it finally reached County Meath, proved an ideal excuse for a party held by Des and Helen in the more spacious home of Larry McGuinness.

Monksfield, at least, was spared the ordeal of parading at Dunmore again. He appeared instead at the even more hazardous Moynalty steam thrashing festival. There, for two miles, he led a procession of ancient steam engines and thrashing machines, prancing proudly, bucking wildly each time the mechanical monster closest behind him let out another high pitched toot. Des McDonogh was invited to sing on stage at the Mullagh village hall and was slightly embarrassed to hear the MC announce, "Now we have a famous television personality to entertain us." He admits, "The whole place was *buzzing* with anticipation at that but it went a bit *flat* when I appeared on the platform."

He sang unaccompanied, for fifteen minutes, crooning bravely despite the sight of the first five rows of seats crammed with children laughing, eating crisps, totally uninterested in his efforts.

Monksfield, meanwhile, enjoyed another summer's rest at grass. One evening his trainer was delayed in Kells; when he returned home he discovered the valuable stable star standing patiently outside the door of his box. Despairing of ever being brought in for his evening feed Monksfield had removed three heavy wooden bars acting as a temporary gate on his paddock and walked calmly back past the bungalow to his box. Using his teeth he had lifted the bars from their sockets and dropped them in a neat pile by the permanent rails.

Monksfield came back into training again early in August with one major objective, to win a second successive Champion Hurdle the following March. His owner and trainer had discussed the idea of retiring him to stud but he continued to show such an extraordinary enthusiasm for racing that their decision to allow him to stay in training for another year was little more than a formality.

Considerable interest had already been shown in Monksfield's future as a stallion. Vincent O'Brien's cigar smoking son-in-law John Magnier, who masterminds a whole bevy of stallions in Ireland under the Coolmore/Castle Hyde umbrella, had written a cryptic letter to Des McDonogh after Cheltenham saying, "Congratulations on winning the Champion Hurdle. Can you please let me know your plans for Monksfield?" A month later another even briefer letter arrived from John Magnier asking, "Please can you let me know your plans for Monksfield's future?"

Both letters were tossed straight into the blazing fire in Des McDonogh's cosy sitting room. An unusual reaction, surely, but he explains, "I did not reply because I thought it was such a rude approach. I have never spoken to the man about the horse and hardly know him. I thought he was very presumptuous, taking a great liberty. No way would Michael Mangan or I want Monksfield to be taken off to someone else's breeding empire at the other end of Ireland for the sole purpose of making money. We don't like the idea of such a fine, brave horse being exploited for monetary gain by a syndicate who might buy him solely for that purpose."

Michael Mangan agrees. He confirms, "When the time comes for Monksfield to go to stud I want his interests to come first. The horse has always come first, not financial implications. I won't have him abused or overworked under any circumstances, certainly not in the way that some stallions are expected to cover a hundred or more mares in a season."

165

Back in training Monksfield's appetite had clearly not been affected by his summer's break; at once he was eating anything from 16 to 19 pounds of nuts a day mixed with additives. He, of course, is the first horse in the yard to be given his breakfast. Des explains, "If I did not feed him first he would make such a tremendous fuss and noise that he would wake the children and then I would be in trouble with Helen." Des had enjoyed feeding the horses when he worked for Helen's father and says, "I still get great satisfaction at seeing empty pots when I go round. When you are directly involved with their exercise as well you know if they need more food. They are fed and watered three times a day and late in the evening I like to go round once more topping up water buckets, checking the horses are all well. Sometimes I wonder why horses are not permanently bored, since they spend so much time merely standing idly in their boxes. Monksfield must just day dream of beating Sea Pigeon and Night Nurse."

Warming to his theme Des McDonogh continued, "Monkey has been the lynch-pin of our lives for the past $5\frac{1}{2}$ years and there will be a big emptiness that will never be filled when he retires. As long as he is at stud and I have some little involvement with him I won't have lost contact altogether. He is everything to us, has put us a little bit on the map and helped us to meet some marvellous people. He's a friend, a companion, like a son to us. If I was a drinking man and had a hangover every Monday morning I'm sure he'd clear it; he puts me in good humour for the rest of the day."

Monksfield is always keen and fresh in the mornings; he bucks, kicks and squeals as he trots up and down the short drive before starting his more serious work. Des McDonogh has often been to the buckle end of the reins, hanging on grimly, but luckily Monksfield does not put down his head too low as he cavorts from one side of the drive to the other.

His curious action wears out racing and normal plates quickly but his patient, skilled blacksmith Kit Bell, recently retired, did not once prick a foot. His successor Liam McAteer, too, has found the horse a placid, sensible character to shoe. "Monksfield", says Joe Brady delightfully, "does not pass any remarks when his feet are being attended to, but he makes plenty

166

of noise when we pull his mane. It grows so quickly it has to be done once a month and he's at his most ticklish then.''

Twice he has been cast in his box, a misleading phrase to describe the situation when a horse rolls in his box and becomes immobile on his back, unable to move, with his legs often trapped between himself and the wall or a manger. Each time Monksfield's roars of discomfort brought helpers who simply pulled him back across his box so that he could stand again.

His legs and tendons have shown not the slightest sign of wear and tear after almost seventy races over a variety of distances on all types of going, fitting testimony to his marvellous constitution. Just once another horse jumped into him in a hurdle race, merely nicking the hairline on his off rear hock.

After 10 weeks in training he was ready for the first of his preparatory runs on the flat, the Irish Cesarewitch at the Curragh on October 7th, ridden by Frank Skelly whose orders to look after his mount were so imprinted on his brain that he hardly dared move throughout the race. The pair, not surprisingly, finished unplaced and did so again three weeks later in another staying handicap at the Curragh.

Des McDonogh now deemed his champion ready to begin the more serious task of hurdling and found the ideal opportunity for his comeback at Down Royal, on November 4th, the A. R. Soudavar Memorial Trial, a conditions hurdle. Injuries once more contributed to the choice of jockey. Tommy Kinane's back was fully recovered but Dessie Hughes had broken an ankle badly in a fall at Listowel in September. So Tommy Kinane rode Monksfield, an even money favourite, to a highly satisfactory $\frac{3}{4}$ length victory over Double Default.

Once again Monksfield was being set impossible tasks by the handicapper but Des McDonogh wanted to give him one more run before attempting to win the Benson and Hedges Handicap Hurdle at Fairyhouse for the second time. He chose the Naas November Handicap, run a week earlier. Humping the steadier of 12 stone, 4 pounds, Monksfield was set to give almost 3 stone to nearly all his rivals yet still finished second to the promising Milan Major who carried a mere 9 stone, 8 pounds. No wonder Milan Major's planned sale to the young English trainer Michael Oliver was swiftly completed. Any horse who had beaten the

167

reigning champion hurdler was unlikely to receive further favours from the handicapper.

The Benson and Hedges Handicap Hurdle proved to be the flash-point of a disagreement between Des McDonogh and Tommy Kinane that grew awkwardly over the next few months. Monksfield, with 12 stone, was once again set a daunting task and had to concede at least 2 stone to all but two of his opponents Fish Quiz (10 stone, 10 pounds) and Rathinree (10 stone, 3 pounds), the horse he had beaten at level weights on the flat in April. Des McDonogh expected Tommy Kinane to ride his usual sensible patient race at Fairyhouse but watched with increasing annoyance as the veteran jockey drove Monksfield into the lead fully four flights from home.

Only Rathinree was able to stay with him. The pair had a sustained battle for the last half mile, first one leading then the other, until an incident at the final hurdle heightened the drama. Rathinree, half a length in front at the time, appeared to jump slightly right handed, hampering Monksfield in the process. Monksfield, in turn, had jumped a little left handed, losing valuable ground as he landed; though he struggled valiantly to regain the leeway he was beaten $1\frac{1}{2}$ lengths. Many observers believed the inevitable Stewards' inquiry would reverse the placings but Des McDonogh did not think so. He says, "I could see no way we were entitled to get the race even though Rathinree did jump slightly to the right, but Tommy was convinced about it. I could not get a word in when he came back to unsaddle because he was complaining and shouting, 'I'll win it in there' pointing to the Stewards' room."

Tommy Kinane confirms, "I was really angry and upset; my horse had run a tremendous race. Rathinree came across me at the last and Monksfield stumbled trying to avoid his hind legs. I knew there was sure to be an inquiry and I told them I deserved to get the race." Once again Tommy came off second best at an important inquiry.

Chaseform Notebook reported more calmly, "Quickening into the last Rathinree jumped it in great style to come away a length clear. The impression that he had taken Monksfield's ground landing on the flat was not borne out by the film view in the Stewards' room and he was a deserving winner."

168

Des McDonogh was furious at the tactics employed on Monksfield. He told Tommy Kinane he had made far too much use of the horse under such a heavy weight and had played into the hands of Tommy McGivern on Rathinree. A dangerous lack of communication seemed to be entering their uneasy partnership. Tommy Kinane, hugely experienced, could be a stubborn man and had always believed it wise to make full use of Monksfield's unlimited stamina. The trainer, however, was displeased at the horse being subjected to an unnecessarily hard race and adds, simply, "It's difficult to give orders to a man 15 years older than myself."

Des contacted Michael Mangan who recalls, "He was critical of Tommy's riding in the Benson and Hedges and said he had made far too much use of the horse. I told him if he wanted to change the jockey then that was the time to do it." A few days later at the races, sufficiently encouraged by Dr Mangan's support, Des met Dessie Hughes, still out of action with a broken ankle, and asked him if he was likely to have a ride in the Champion Hurdle still $3\frac{1}{2}$ months away. Hughes, who had never ridden in the race, laughed as he shook his head, and agreed to stand by to ride Monksfield. It was not a firm booking, more a tentative approach to ensure he was available if needed.

The former Royal flat race jockey Harry Carr, writing in his syndicated column, voiced the anxieties of many of Monksfield's supporters at the time: "My only worry is that he could get worn out along the way. Fairyhouse was the sixty-second race of his career and I wonder how much longer he can continue to give oceans of weight away to youthful stars such as Rathinree."

Further accolades were still being collected by Monksfield's connections. Des McDonogh and Michael Mangan won the Sean Graham 1978 awards, selected by the overwhelming vote of the Irish Racing Writers Association as the National Hunt Trainer and Owner of the Year. Tommy Kinane, too, was chosen to receive a special award for his part in Monksfield's Champion Hurdle triumph. At a reception at Leopardstown the three men each received a fine framed coloured print of Monksfield jumping the last hurdle at Cheltenham in the lead, though Des McDonogh, busy riding out at home, arrived rather late to collect his picture. A week later he was voted Sports Personality of Limerick, 1978, and duly accepted another trophy at the Limerick Inn Hotel. Des and Helen were also guests of honour at a dinner given by the Meath Regional group of breeders to mark Monksfield's achievements.

The final week before Christmas proved a time of agonizing indecision for Des McDonogh. A meeting in Northern Ireland, at which he hoped to run Monksfield five days before Christmas was called off late in the morning. Should he then send Monksfield to England on Boxing Day for the William Hill Hurdle, a race which offered ideal weight conditions; or should he run him instead in the Irish Sweeps Handicap Hurdle a day later at Leopardstown when once again he would have to give lumps of weight to useful rivals? A second problem was even more awkward. Dessie Hughes' ankle had finally mended and he was hoping to make a comeback at that very Leopardstown meeting but it would hardly be fair to ask a jockey who was not fully fit to ride Monksfield in such an important race. So despite the trainer's dissatisfaction at Fairyhouse Tommy Kinane kept the mount.

Des McDonogh preferred Kempton but the weather was so bad at home he thought it must change. Christmas would be an awkward time to move people around for, naturally, they would prefer to be with their families. He had to think of the possibility of travelling to England then finding Kempton races cancelled by bad weather while racing was able to go ahead in Ireland.

In the end he chose to run the horse at Leopardstown but after watching on television Kybo beat Birds Nest at Kempton Des admits, "I was so depressed that I had not gone to England." The going at Kempton had been good, with ideal conditions. The same could certainly not be said of Leopardstown where torrential rain had turned the course into a vast lake. Few, if any, English racecourses would even have considered attempting to race in such dreadful conditions but there was no question at all of the meeting being postponed. Des McDonogh and Michael Mangan considered withdrawing Monksfield but eventually agreed he should run, safe in the knowledge that Tommy Kinane had promised to look after the horse throughout the race.

Tommy recalls, "I thought Des would withdraw the horse

Monksfield and Des McDonogh on a bitterly cold
morning in December 1978.          *Credit: Chris Smith*

but I'm glad he didn't because he was in tremendous form that day; almost the best I've ever ridden him. *Sparkling* form! My instructions were to mind him and I did just that." Monksfield ran a magnificent race; well placed from the start he threatened to take the lead briefly on the final bend and was only beaten into third place by the enormous weight concession to the first two, Chinrullah and Glassilaun. Poor Dessie Hughes missed a valuable win on Chinrullah for he had broken his thumb when a horse stood on his hand as he fell on his comeback ride, Chestnut Belle, half an hour before the Irish Sweeps.

Des McDonogh, who had severely criticized his jockey at Fairyhouse, now comments, "Tommy did his job well and did not knock the horse about. I thought Monksfield ran a hell of a race and had earned a little holiday so for the next two weeks he did nothing strong at all, just tootling about. He did himself too well, became a bit unfit and the next thing we were snowed up for six long weeks. It was the worst winter of all."

# 18

# Winter of Discontent

Monksfield *hated* the cold. Several rugs and blankets on his back at night failed to lift his spirits. Des McDonogh even tried a heat ray lamp in his box but took it away after only two nights because he feared it might be affecting the horse's eyes. Snow lay 8, sometimes 10 inches deep on the fields of Billywood; the horses cantered gingerly in different places each day since their tracks would freeze overnight. Monksfield was able to go only 2 furlongs uphill on fresh snow, pull up, walk back down and canter up again. There was no question of any horse being able to exercise over a longer distance.

In desperation Des McDonogh bought 450 bales of straw at 40 pence each and spread them thickly enough to make a short canter along the length of his biggest field. After three days pounding, earth, snow and straw were frozen together solidly and he had to look elsewhere to work his horses. In mid-January, 10 days in advance, he sent off the entry form for a suitable trial race at Wolverhampton for Monksfield. One of the many sudden postal strikes in Ireland ensured it did not arrive in time.

Often he would box up four or five horses to take them the two miles or so to the field owned by Larry McGuinness. There, at least, the snow was not quite so deep; if he waited until the brief daily thaw in the early afternoon the trainer was able to work Monksfield and his stable companions in safety around the edge of the field.

Des McDonogh became more anxious as the weeks passed. He knew he was well behind schedule and comments, "I was worried like hell. Monkey was not even half straight. We were counting the days yet at one stage the weather was so bad we felt Cheltenham could not possibly be on. There was no sign of a change. The freeze just went on and on."

Monksfield's next planned race, weather permitting, was the Erin Foods Hurdle at Leopardstown on February 24th. Another postal strike added to the problems of Irish trainers so Des McDonogh set off valiantly in his car in a snowstorm early one evening to deliver the Erin Foods entry form by hand at the Curragh, usually no more than an hour and a half away. Creeping along the hard packed snow he reached the deserted white wasteland of the Curragh after four hours, handed in the entry form and set off on the arduous return journey to Billywood at speeds that varied between 15 and 20 m.p.h. One late night driver was brave enough to overtake him. Less than a mile further on Des found the impetuous skirmisher clambering out of the window of his car which was lying upside down in a ditch.

Two weeks before the Erin Foods, desperate to give Monksfield some stronger work, the McDonoghs drove eight miles on the ice packed roads to Balrathbury, home of the brilliant international showjumper Eddie Macken and his wife Suzanne, to ask if they might breeze the horse in their indoor riding school. The Mackens were only too pleased to help. Des recalls, "We cantered Monkey and Stranfield round and round, both ways, for about an hour until we were blue in the face. It was tremendous to keep them moving but the school was a bit tight for Monksfield, two bounds and he was at the end."

A few days later, knowing Monksfield was still far from race fitness, Des rang Mick O'Toole who readily agreed that he could bring the champion over for a session in his large circular covered ride, a furlong round. It took Des three hours to drive the horse-box to O'Toole's stable on the edge of the Curragh; when he arrived there he found the trainer watching films of old races on his television video. The two men enjoyed the sight of Monksfield winning the 1978 Champion Hurdle yet again, then, suitably inspired, Mick O'Toole put on his boots, opened up the indoor school and helped saddle Monksfield.

Des McDonogh raises an eyebrow as he reports, "Mick told me what he did with his horses in there and I doubled it!" Monksfield covered eight laps, a mile, left handed accompanied

174

by Stranfield then completed another six laps, alone, right handed. Mick O'Toole, watching with considerable interest, suggested Des might also like to canter Monksfield round his huge field as the snow had almost melted there. Dessie Hughes jumped on Stranfield to show the way and the two horses covered a further mile in the softened ground.

The Erin Foods Hurdle at Leopardstown proved to be the most controversial of Monksfield's career. His trainer felt the horse would run well but was not fit enough to win. He comments, "He had to need the run because we had not been able to give him enough work. In the parade ring I told Tommy to give the horse a chance, to hold him up a bit more than usual and not to hit the front too early as he had done there before." Normally at Leopardstown he felt the horse was burned up before he reached a small ridge a furlong and a half from the line; and he told Tommy he did not mind whether the horse won or not provided he saved Monksfield for the second half of the race and so was running on at the finish.

Warm favourite for the Erin Foods at 5/4 was the English trained Major Thompson who had only just been beaten in the Schweppes Hurdle at Newbury a fortnight earlier under top weight of 12 stone. Monksfield was next in the betting at 5/2 but from his point of view the race was a disaster. None of the jockeys wanted to make the running so the field crawled along at a funeral pace, barely fast enough to jump the first two flights of hurdles. At the back of the bunch Monksfield could be seen pulling furiously for his head. The runners sauntered leisurely past the stands and out into the country until John Harty quickened the pace dramatically by forcing Exalted into a clear lead. Towards the rear Monksfield, caught out by the sudden acceleration, was suddenly struggling in vain to stay in touch.

In the stands Des McDonogh was furious. "Tommy had been lockjawing Monkey, hauling him back and back. I could not understand it. I could not run down off the stands and tell him they were going too slow." Jockeys are expected to use their initiative when a race is run differently than expected. Preconceived tactics can and should be ditched if necessary. Tommy Kinane, however, chose to remain at the back of the field despite the obvious lack of pace. Defiantly he argues, "At the start

175

Monksfield wanted to go but I pulled him back and after that he was never happy. I had to carry out my instructions to ride a waiting race but after the third hurdle when I wanted to make a move he just would not go in the sticky ground."

Whatever the reason Monksfield was left behind with the stragglers as the race developed many lengths ahead of him. Jonjo O'Neill, making ground steadily on Major Thompson, passed Monksfield at the fourth last hurdle and remembers, "He was going nowhere. Absolutely nowhere. The way he was running it looked as though he would finish tailed off."

Exalted led until early in the straight but was swamped as Connaught Ranger and Major Thompson came bursting through at the last flight. On the flat Connaught Ranger strode clear to win impressively by 5 lengths from Major Thompson with Monksfield, running on as ever at the finish, beaten some 16 lengths into sixth place. Des McDonogh, unusually pale and

Time for straight talking. Tommy Kinane and Des McDonogh agree to disagree.     *Credit: Ruth Rogers*

tense, muttered to waiting reporters, "That's only the second bad race he's run in his life. The slow early pace and dead ground did not help but you can't print what I really think. The man on top should have pushed up a lot earlier."

Tommy Kinane, grim faced, spoke briefly to the trainer before disappearing to change for his next ride. Much later the two men spent an hour in animated and at times heated conversation outside the weighing room. Des McDonogh had been annoyed because Tommy Kinane had made too much use of Monksfield at Fairyhouse and now he made it clear he was furious because the horse had been given far too much to do in the Erin Foods. Clearly their fluctuating relationship had reached crisis point.

Pressure on Des McDonogh increased daily. The Champion Hurdle was only $2\frac{1}{2}$ weeks away, the horse was still not fully fit and the rift with his jockey had become irreparable. Blood tests taken immediately after the Erin Foods showed Monksfield to be slightly anaemic so he was put on a short course of folic acid. Communication with Michael Mangan in Newfoundland seemed impossible thanks to the industrial action taken by postal workers; but through the faithful Jack Kelsey Dr Mangan had heard of Monksfield's poor display at Leopardstown and of the subsequent disagreement between jockey and trainer. Michael Mangan is a kind, generous, good-natured man but he was not prepared to allow his horse, such a gallant and popular Champion, to be involved in a long-drawn-out public wrangle so he wrote a lengthy considered letter to Des McDonogh and sent it by hand with a friend who was flying to Ireland.

In the letter Dr Mangan instructed that if the horse was not fit enough then he should not run at Cheltenham. He confirms, "I was quite prepared to miss Cheltenham, and wait until Monksfield was 100 per cent for Liverpool and other races a little later. I also said in the letter if Des thought Tommy Kinane could ride Monksfield as well as Dessie Hughes he should keep him. If not it was his duty to the horse and to myself to retain Dessie Hughes. I added my own view that it would be a totally different race from 1978, without an obvious pacemaker like Night Nurse, and that if my preference were taken into account it would have to be Dessie Hughes. I gave Des all the options."

The two men were then able to speak by telephone thanks to a complicated system, arranged by Jack Kelsey, involving the use of friends' telephones and synchronized timing. Des McDonogh assured Michael Mangan the horse would be fit to run at Cheltenham and, after further discussion, the decision was taken to replace Tommy Kinane with Dessie Hughes. The biggest single factor in their choice was the knowledge that Monksfield would almost certainly have to make his own running, a task that would require perfect judgement of pace and timing by an experienced big-race jockey. Tommy Kinane, though he knew the horse so well, had ridden only three winners since Monksfield's previous success early in November. Dessie Hughes, in contrast, was in tremendous form including a treble at the Erin Foods meeting. Dr Mangan also felt it was foolish of Tommy Kinane to have taken a spare ride on a complete outsider which had fallen in the steeplechase before the Erin Foods. Paddy Broderick, he reasoned, had given up riding over fences to ensure he would be fit to ride Night Nurse, and he believed Monksfield deserved the same courtesy from his jockey.

Perhaps if Des McDonogh had been a harder, more ruthless and cold-blooded man, he might have avoided the controversy that erupted over the changing of Monksfield's jockey. Certainly he would have been wiser to have settled the matter after the Benson and Hedges Hurdle at Fairyhouse early in December rather than delaying the decision until the eve of Cheltenham. But the very unusual qualities that have made him such an outstanding trainer of Monksfield caused him to shy away from the fateful moment of change. Quite simply he kept postponing the inevitable. The lack of telephone and postal facilities had not helped. No doubt if Dr Mangan had lived in Ireland or the telephones had been working normally the problem would have been solved much earlier. But lack of communication was not an insurmountable obstacle. In the end the decision was Michael Mangan's but it was one the trainer both agreed with and desired.

Des McDonogh told Tommy Kinane the bad news at Leopardstown on March 7th, exactly a week before the Champion Hurdle. It did not come as a complete shock, for rumours of a change had been sweeping Ireland since the Erin Foods and the

178

*Sunday People* had carried a story four days earlier predicting the move.

Tommy Kinane, deeply hurt, comments, "No way was I entitled to be jocked off. I was disgusted and felt like throwing the whole thing in. That was the first time in my life I decided I was going to give up. I don't understand why it happened and as far as I am concerned I am still entitled to ride the horse. Des has trained Monksfield brilliantly. The proof is there. But he and I were not good at discussing things. I'm still bitter and sore and when I got home that day I felt like taking down all the photographs of Monksfield and throwing them away but that would not have been fair to the horse. He has given me some great moments."

Tommy Kinane, understandably, remains upset at losing the ride on Monksfield. But he was and is a freelance jockey, and at no stage was retained or paid a retainer to ride the horse. Further piquancy was added to the situation by the fact that Des McDonogh planned to run Stranfield in a valuable novice hurdle at the Cheltenham meeting. Tommy Kinane was his regular jockey, too. The trainer could have taken the easy course and replaced him on Stranfield but he explains, "Tommy had done nothing wrong on the horse so as far as I was concerned he deserved to ride him at Cheltenham."

Monksfield, meanwhile, his anaemia cured, had been doing an enormous amount of steady exercise. Des McDonogh admits, "I suppose I worked hell out of him more often in a week than I really would have liked." Several times he galloped round Larry McGuinness' field and he paid a second visit to Eddie Macken's indoor school. He also worked sometimes in another large field owned by Matt Gilsenan, former captain of Meath Football Team. On the Friday before Cheltenham Des took Monksfield and Lisdu to gallop at the Curragh. Mick O'Toole once again helped by choosing the right place to work them and he also offered the considerable services of the leading flat race jockey Tony Murray to partner Lisdu while Dessie Hughes rode Monksfield.

Dessie Hughes was delighted at the thought of riding Monksfield in the Champion Hurdle. He says, "I could not turn the ride down simply because I was very fond of Tommy and we had been friends for a good few years. Already I had been getting huge bonuses out of the horse which would have been his if he had not been hurt. But I'm a professional. When you have struggled as long as me and then start to get good rides there's no way you can refuse an offer like that through sentiment. When it happened Tommy was very peeved and I don't blame him; he did not speak to me in the weighing room even though we sat next to each other. But it was just a face he was putting on in front of other people. Basically he knew it was not my fault and down at the start and in a race he was as friendly as ever. In the weighing room and round other people he was trying to make out he did not like me at all and I was after doing a terrible wrong to him."

Dessie Hughes was not impressed with Monksfield during their work out at the Curragh on the Friday. He recalls, "He went terrible, really bad, never took hold of his bridle, was not going fast and all the while Lisdu was cantering over us. He did not seem a bit interested in working and slowed to look at every furlong marker."

Des McDonogh, more used to his horse's lazy habits at home, was not too concerned. Although Monksfield was certainly not impressive that morning he knew the horse was at last coming to himself. He confirms, "The time of the year is the most vital factor for him. Because of the weather we knew he was not as ready for Cheltenham as in the previous years but neither, we suspected, were the other horses in England and Ireland. Gradually I had felt the sparkle coming back in him. Dessie may not have thought it was there but I knew it was because I had been riding him at home every day."

The next day, Saturday, Monksfield completed his Cheltenham preparation trotting and cantering four miles on the roads. On his way home, his trainer noted happily, the horse was bucking and kicking joyously, as full of life and energy as a 2-year-old. Monksfield and Stranfield travelled over to England on Sunday with Des McDonogh and Joe Brady in attendance, leaving Helen to supervise the stable's two runners at Roscommon on the Monday.

# 19

# Champion again

The build-up in the final tense days before the 1979 Champion Hurdle proved to be the most controversial in the race's long history. Some Irish papers, without bothering to check the facts, had reacted to the news of Tommy Kinane's replacement with vicious criticism of Monksfield's owner and trainer. In England a series of false rumours circulated hinting that Monksfield's great rival Sea Pigeon, at the time ante-post favourite for the race, was not fit to run. *The Sporting Life* added fuel to the flames by running an inaccurate scare story across five columns at the top of page one.

Under the headline "Is Sea Pigeon Fit?" the article was based on a report that the horse had broken a blood vessel during his narrow defeat by Decent Fellow in his final outing before Cheltenham. Some bookies were said to have suspended betting on the Champion Hurdle.

The story continued, "The mystery deepened when a spokesman for the Easterby stable and the 8-year-old's owner Pat Muldoon both provided cryptic and evasive answers when questioned point blank about the gelding's well-being. When asked, 'Will Sea Pigeon run, and is he well?' the Easterby spokesman replied, 'You can say he will run'.

"Muldoon was similarly coy when put the identical question. He chuckled, 'Frankly that's classified information. But he definitely runs.'"

*The Sporting Life* report continued, "Once the fitness question was stutteringly dealt with the Easterby spokesman loosened up and admitted that 'He vaguely remembered Sea Pigeon bursting a blood vessel when he was three or four – but only then.'"

"With Sea Pigeon forever humping huge weights and running in sticky ground it would come as no surprise to find that a blood vessel has cracked under such pressure. Bearing this in mind," said the eager hack with massive authority, "and the horse's widespread favouritism for the Champion – now 7/2 – at least some doubt must be placed on his absolute fitness and the public might be wise to remember this when preparing for a plunge."

Sea Pigeon's gallant performance at Cheltenham effectively nailed that damaging innuendo and an embarrassing postscript followed this sorry tale. Four days later, on the morning of the Champion Hurdle, *The Sporting Life* carried two terse paragraphs stating they had since learned Pat Muldoon was not the man who spoke to the newspaper. They apologized and regretted any embarrassment caused.

Far from being coy and evasive the genial Pat Muldoon has always gone to considerable lengths to help racing writers and reporters with facts and opinions about his horses in training. Surprised by all the scare stories he said "Sea Pigeon blew and *heaved* so much after his last race there was a slight trace of blood. That's all. I have never been so confident of winning at Cheltenham. If it's not his year this time it never will be. It's a two-horse race again and if we are beaten Sea Pigeon will be remembered as the best horse never to win the Champion Hurdle."

Muldoon based his optimism on the expected good going, a planned change in tactics, and a firmly held view that the difference between Jonjo O'Neill, who knew Sea Pigeon so well, and another top-class jockey, Frank Berry, who had ridden him in 1978, would make up the two lengths by which he was beaten the previous year.

By 1979 Muldoon, a wholesale wine importer, had eleven horses in training. His business pressure was so intense that he believed it was vital to have another interest to remain sane. He says, "The cost of buying horses can be pretty steep, and I write that off, but so far their running costs and training bills have been covered by prize money. Of course the luck to own a warrior like Sea Pigeon comes once in a lifetime. He has subsidized some of the others."

Muldoon, then, was bullishly confident the weekend before Cheltenham but Des McDonogh, too, was much happier about Monksfield's chances. He had three mornings left to complete his preparation and believed his horse might be just as ready as all the others held up by the extended winter. On Monday morning he worked Monksfield steadily over two miles at little more than half-speed and returned to his hotel thoroughly satisfied with his horse's condition. A series of phone calls early in the afternoon shattered that contentment. Reporters from London began ringing to ask if it was true that Monksfield was lame and unlikely to run in the Champion Hurdle, then only 48 hours away.

Des recalls, "I had an awful *fright* at the first call and turned white as a sheet. The way Monkey had pulled and galloped that morning hardly suggested anything was wrong, and I knew Joe would have contacted me if something had happened after I left the stables." Reporters, by nature, are a hard-headed, disbelieving breed. One newspaper even rang twice in five minutes despite the trainer's categorical denial that Monksfield was lame. By the end of the afternoon Des McDonogh, his patience worn down, had devised an admirably short, accurate, fitting and unprintable one word reply to Fleet Street's newshounds. At evening stables he was relieved to discover Monksfield in his usual perky form.

Des was waiting quietly in the bar of his hotel later that evening when he overheard a conversation between four men nearby which seemed to hint that Monksfield's behaviour at home was less than perfect. There was a suggestion that mares were smuggled into his box in the middle of the night for his pleasure ... worse, that he had been seen, by a reliable source, masturbating in his box. Des McDonogh, intensely proud and justifiably protective of his horse, butted angrily into their conversation, and told the astonished group, "That's a *disgusting* thing to say about a great horse. I've never heard of or seen a horse do that. It's utter nonsense and you all ought to be ashamed of yourselves!" A potentially explosive situation was averted by a call for Des McDonogh to answer a phone call at reception. The four men, suddenly aware of the identity of the interloper, wriggled in embarrassment and when the call was finished insisted on buying him a large orange juice.

Next morning after working Monksfield over two miles, the trainer returned to his hotel to discover that *The Sporting Life*, at least, had not believed his statement the previous evening.

Under the huge headline, "No Monksfield? Nonsense, says McDonogh", the story blazed across page one on the day before the Champion Hurdle began "Persistent rumours that Monksfield will not run in tomorrow's Champion Hurdle were hotly denied by the trainer Des McDonogh last night.

"He told me firmly, 'I rode the horse myself this morning and he is perfectly OK. I saw him at 6 p.m. and he was in great shape. He is certain to run'.

"However rumours that he 'pulled up feelingly after yesterday's spin and has heat in his joints' were rife in London." The writer then added he would not have a penny on the reigning champion until he saw him canter down sound to the start. He continued, "Connections, understandably, are desperately keen to run the brave 7-year-old, who is sure to be scrutinized minutely when he walks out of his box this morning."

It is history now that the two horses reported by *The Sporting Life* to be invalids fought out a memorable duel in the Champion Hurdle the length of Fleet Street ahead of the rest of the field. The newspapers also carried better news from Roscommon that Des McDonogh had come close to his first double under National Hunt rules; Lisdu, ridden by Frank Skelly, had won there and in another race Off Target had finished second, beaten by only three-quarters of a length. Later on Tuesday Des was interviewed on television for the first time and Helen arrived to join him for their ritual Champion Hurdle dinner with Michael Mangan and his friends at their favourite Italian restaurant in Gloucester.

Early on Wednesday Monksfield, ridden by Des McDonogh, and Stranfield, ridden by Helen, worked together over a mile and three-quarters to the astonished fascination of a gaggle of professional observers standing in the driving rain. Dismissing the final gallop as no more than a routine pipe-opener Des insists, "We went about three and a half times round, steadier than the previous two days and then a little faster up the centre of the track at the finish; perhaps a mile and a half steady then two and a half furlongs a bit quicker but still on the bridle. I just

184

wanted to loosen them up and stick to the system I had used in previous years."

Several watching pundits took a substantially different view. Trainers, jockeys and reporters alike were amazed at such a strenuous exercise gallop only hours before both horses were due to run. Joe Rowntree standing with several Northern jockeys and trainers later wrote in the Irish *Evening Herald*, "Monksfield and Stranfield completed the most punishing pre-race gallop I have ever known. Together the pair covered more than 10 furlongs in heavy ground and at a real swinging pace before pulling up, blowing hard. That's it, I thought, surely Monksfield cannot win now, and when I was told he had done the same thing the morning before a thick black line went through his name on my racecard. This man McDonogh must be mad, I told all and sundry. The sight made Sea Pigeon something of a certainty."

Joe Rowntree has never been afraid to air his views in public and there were plenty of people, less forthright perhaps, who agreed with his summing-up. All of them simply failed to understand the extraordinarily close, almost psychic, relationship between Monksfield and his trainer. One man who certainly did appreciate Des McDonogh's qualities was Peter Easterby, trainer of Sea Pigeon. As the champion walked jauntily back to the racecourse stables after that famous final gallop Peter looked closely at his powerful quarters and nodded to Des, "My God, he's not that small. When are you going to retire him to stud and give someone else a chance?"

The going on Champion Hurdle day was desperately heavy. Persistent rain in the previous two days had drastically reduced the chances of horses needing good ground to produce their best form. Times on the opening day Tuesday had been agonizingly slow; Venture to Cognac had won the first race of the meeting in a time 48 seconds slower than average. Master Smudge, successful in the 3 mile Sun Alliance Chase, had taken almost a minute longer than the average time and further rain overnight had not given the course a chance to dry out. Lunching on a pork pie and a glass of orange on Wednesday Des McDonogh was concerned that the going would be far too soft for Stranfield in the opening race, the Waterford Crystal Supreme Novice Hurdle, though his race, at least, would help to ease the pressure of events later in the afternoon. In the paddock Tommy Kinane, serious, dour, unsmiling, listened with professional intent as Des McDonogh told him to hold up Stranfield as long as possible, last of all for the first half of the race to conserve his powerful finishing sprint. When Des had given Tommy the same instructions on Stranfield's first run over hurdles the veteran jockey had asked quizzically, "Are you fancying him today?" They had won in a canter from a useful field that day but had not been successful since.

Fluctuating in the betting market Stranfield eventually settled at 16/1 while the Irish plunged on Corrib Chieftain and Glassilaun. Riding exactly to orders Tommy Kinane settled Stranfield in the rear in the early stages, brought him with a promising run on the wide outside down the hill and to his intense glee, passed the leader Dessie Hughes on Killamonan in the air at the final flight and sprinted 5 lengths clear on the run–in despite veering sharply left–handed.

Stranfield (Tommy Kinane), sweeps past Killamonan
(Dessie Hughes) on the way to an easy victory in the
Waterford Crystal Supreme Novice Hurdle. *Credit: George Selwyn*

Tommy admits, "I rode Stranfield in a temper. I wanted to show them they were wrong to take me off Monksfield. I answered my critics. I did it out of pure temper and made Stranfield a super horse on the day. He has a lot more speed than Monksfield but would not fight like him." Carried away by his easy victory Tommy Kinane returned on Stranfield shouting, "I'm not beat yet. They can't keep a good man down," and was given a warm reception in the winner's enclosure. Tommy Kinane's victory had quite definitely added a delicate edge to the proceedings but Dessie Hughes helped to restore some sort of equilibrium by winning the second race, the Arkle Challenge Trophy, on Chinrullah.

The McDonoghs, acutely aware of the rising tension, were surrounded by crowds of well-wishers and onlookers as they walked out to saddle Monksfield. Helen, in particular, was convinced they could not have two winners in an afternoon. "It might happen to a big trainer but not to us," she reasoned gloomily. Des was a little more confident. "I knew I had the best horse in the world going out to battle for me."

Even in the pouring rain Monksfield's coat glistened brightly. Dessie Hughes, who had walked the course and had the benefit of a ride in the first hurdle race, explained that he would take the same wide route on Monksfield in search of the faster strip of ground he had found there earlier. As Dessie Hughes mounted Monksfield the most alert spectators packed twenty deep round the paddock might have spotted Michael Mangan enact a strange ritual. Touching Monksfield lightly on the head with the relic of a Lebanese Saint he intoned quite seriously in Arabic, "Run, Your Highness." Dr Mangan was fulfilling a promise to his great friend Dr Falah Maroun, a neuro-surgeon who had been unable to make the trip to Cheltenham.

The driving rain had caused Sea Pigeon to drift ominously in the market from his position of ante-post favourite early in the week right out to 6/1. Monksfield was heavily backed down to 9/4 favourite with significant support at 4/1 for the rising star Kybo, winner of his three previous races including two valuable prizes at Ascot and the William Hill Hurdle at Kempton. Western Rose, too, was a 6/1 chance, with his stable companion Connaught Ranger at 10/1 despite his victory in the Erin Foods

Battle is joined. A marvellous sequence of photographs by George Selwyn captures the unforgettable duel between Monksfield and Sea Pigeon at the last hurdle in the 1979 Champion Hurdle. *Credit: George Selwyn*

Hurdle. Rank outsider at 500/1 in the field of ten was the small filly River Belle who in her final race before Cheltenham had finished nearly last carrying only 10 stone, 2 pounds in a modest handicap at Hereford. This did not deter her optimistic owner-trainer Henry Ford from backing her to win £125,000 in the Champion Hurdle.

Unfortunately for Henry Ford, River Belle was already struggling to stay in touch as Monksfield led Beacon Light,

Kybo and Sea Pigeon out into the country while a second group chose to go on the shorter route on the inside. River Belle was tailed off by the time Monksfield started the downhill run that suits him so well and it soon became apparent that only those who had followed him on the wide outside were able to stay in touch, for on the inside Western Rose, Birds Nest and Connaught Ranger were already beaten. The champion landed two lengths clear over the third last but Kybo was close behind, and Sea Pigeon was moving ominously well.

Together in the air at the last hurdle. Note Jonjo O'Neill grinning confidently on Sea Pigeon while Dessie Hughes is hard at work on Monksfield.

*Credit: George Selwyn*

189

The dramatic fall of Kybo at the penultimate hurdle for a moment left Monksfield several lengths clear but then Sea Pigeon simply cruised up to join him, moving so easily that it seemed just a question of when Jonjo O'Neill would let him stride on to an overdue victory. Monksfield's most fervent admirers cannot deny that in the next few seconds their hero appeared to be heading for certain defeat at the hands of his speedier rival.

On the final bend, scrambling to gain more purchase on the worst of the ground, he seemed to lose his action completely,

Coming away from the hurdle Jonjo is still laughing but Monksfield will not accept defeat. Note how the Champion lays back his ears in his determination to pass his great rival. *Credit: George Selwyn*

190

Locked together. The two horses and jockeys on the steep
uphill finish.                                  *Credit: George Selwyn*

floundered for a moment as he became unbalanced, then quickened valiantly as if tied by an invisible thread to Sea Pigeon's
quarters. The two combatants both jumped the last hurdle quite
brilliantly yet somehow the reigning champion managed to
regain a valuable yard and a half as he landed far out at the very
foot of the final, daunting hill. Now the pair were joined in a
deadly battle of consuming intensity. At first Jonjo O'Neill was
still smiling as Sea Pigeon remained perhaps a neck in front but
slowly, painfully, inexorably Monksfield clawed his way back
into contention, and then fought his way into the lead. He surged
on towards the winning post and reached it three-quarters of a
length before his demoralized victim.

191

Joe Brady, glum faced, tight lipped, ran up miserably to catch Monksfield. Only when Jonjo O'Neill trotted over to shake hands with Dessie Hughes did Joe smile. "Did you win?" he asked before exploding in a frenzy of excitement.

Dessie Hughes, overwhelmed at the experience, insists, "I've never ridden in a race for everything to go so well. Insignificant things can happen that cost you half a length or so but that day everything worked perfectly. He met every hurdle spot on. If the race was run again I don't think I would have won on him because surely something, however minor, would have gone wrong. He could not have done it perfectly again and only his unique brand of courage enabled him to do it at all."

Up in the stands Des McDonogh felt completely deflated in the last ten strides as the tension drained out of him. He says, "The last three hurdles were sheer ecstasy to watch, an extra-ordinary emotional experience unlike anything else I have known in my life. When I saw Monkey draw clear in the last ten strides I hugged Michael Mangan unashamedly."

Tommy Kinane, close to tears, stayed in the anonymity of the jockeys changing room. Six months later in the comfort of his own home he choked back the emotion and was unable to speak for thirty seconds as he remembered the bitter sweetness of Cheltenham. Eventually he whispered haltingly, "I was wronged . . . and I've still not given up hope of getting back on Monksfield. I'd have beaten him if I had ridden Sea Pigeon. I could have told them exactly how to beat Monksfield. Instead they played right into his hands and allowed Sea Pigeon to get into a long battle with him. You've got to come and beat Monksfield quickly and late so that he does not have enough time to fight back."

Monksfield returned to a tumultuous reception. Mick O'Toole, tears flowing down his cheeks, ran out to pat the Champion's quarters. Dozens of people unconnected with the horse managed to push, squeeze and wheedle their way into the winner's enclosure. Des and Helen McDonogh, bursting with pride, were completely cut off from their horse but Pat Muldoon forced his way through the enclosing ring and, unable to speak, put his arms round Des. His actions spoke louder than words.

Arthur Ryan, who had looked after Monksfield for the first

192

two years of his life, had felt guilty about risking his first visit to Cheltenham for years, since he had seen the horse run half a dozen times without winning and was afraid the sequence might continue. He and his wife Elizabeth watched the race from the packed lawn in front of the monstrous new concrete grandstand, saw Monksfield jump the last hurdle, then sprinted to cheer him into the winner's enclosure.

A fortnight later a case of whisky arrived unexpectedly at the Ryans' home at Inch. When I called there in late summer it was still unopened, gathering dust with most of his correspondence. Arthur Ryan thought it might have been an award for his cattle, or perhaps from a race Monksfield had won sponsored by a whisky firm. It was, in fact, the monthly breeders' prize from *Pacemaker* magazine for March 1979.

# 20

# The Monksfield Hurdle

Monksfield's triumph was the third Irish win in succession that afternoon following Stranfield and Chinrullah. When the ovation eventually dimmed a comedian in the crowd lining the unsaddling enclosure shouted, "How are the English doing at the other meeting?"

In the mêlée before the presentations someone asked Des McDonogh if he had been worried when Sea Pigeon had headed Monksfield. "Not at all," he replied, adding with a broad smile, "Sure we only wanted to give the other fellow a bit of pleasure."

Away in another corner of the unsaddling enclosure Peter Easterby was heard to observe drily, "It's a pity pigeons cannot swim."

On his way into the jockeys' changing room Dessie Hughes passed Tommy Kinane, visibly upset. He recalls, "I just caught Tommy's eye and I did feel for him. It was very touching. He really felt it when I walked in and so did I. There's no doubt I had to win on the horse to justify the switch. The pressure was on me after Stranfield had won."

Later when Tommy Kinane was leaving the course, he met Des McDonogh. At first unable to speak the two men shook hands silently before Tommy whispered, "I would have won on him too," and walked quietly away.

Back in the villages surrounding Kells, Des McDonogh's first double under National Hunt rules was greeted with wild celebrations. The post and telephone strike prevented many villagers in Mullagh sending their bets through to the local bookies in Kells. Who better to deliver them than Mrs Jenny McNamee, the warm, plump, homely landlady of their favourite bar in Mullagh? Virtually the whole village backed Monksfield and many of them included Stranfield in doubles. The kind hearted Jenny McNamee set off at lunchtime for the Kells betting shop, her handbag bulging with notes of all descriptions and handfuls of silver.

Perhaps £700 or £800 went on Monksfield that day from Mullagh alone and when Mrs McNamee returned to her bar in time to watch Stranfield's race she found it packed to overflowing. "You could barely move," she reports with glee. "The lads were standing ten deep and the way they lifted Monkey home here with their voices, sure he did not need a jockey away there at Cheltenham." A huge photo of Monksfield dwarfs the bar. Time and smoke have aged it prematurely but she will not hear of it being taken down. Mrs McNamee, no doubt, also plunged on Monksfield that fateful day for soon afterwards a brand new video recording machine was added to the attractions of her smart bar in the main street of Mullagh.

Larry McGuinness, too, recounts with considerable relish tales of bookmakers crying for mercy after Stranfield and Monksfield had both won. "Sure many of the boys had a little fiver double the two. All the people who stayed at home this year doubled the two horses. The local bookies were crippled. Several of them were badly bent if not completely broken. The man in Kells in particular got a fearful scorching from the punters in Mullagh. When Monkey goes to England dozens of people from round here go because they know he'll pay for their fare. He's their free passport to England."

Late in the autumn of 1979 we sat in the drawing-room of Larry McGuinness' large house and listened again to the immaculate tones of Peter O'Sullevan, on tape, commentating on Stranfield and Monksfield winning their races. The final pulsating seconds of each finish were completely drowned by the joyous shouting, cheering and hollering as the McGuinness family and their friends roared the pair home.

Celebrations in Cheltenham, too, were prolonged. Michael Mangan threw yet another lavish dinner party at his hotel with the usual speeches, song and poems in honour of the great dual champion hurdler. After breakfast the next morning the

McDonoghs called in on the Mangans' room and found the daily newspapers, opened at the racing pages, spread over the bed.

Des recalls, "That was a marvellous moment because I think it was then they realized what we had done. Unless you lived in Mullagh I don't think you could begin to appreciate the problems we had suffered with the weather in the previous 11 weeks."

The Irish *Evening Herald* carried a magnanimous slice of humble pie from Joe Rowntree, beginning, "This is an epistle from an Englishman in Cheltenham, dazed, disappointed and frustrated after 2 days of trying to untangle the Irish logic and weigh up their racing machines. For, after watching Monksfield retain his title yesterday, now I can do no more than hold up my hands, admit I was wrong and tell Des McDonogh that he's a great trainer. Both his runners were turned out immaculately and he has a tremendous record at the meeting. Monksfield is a worthy champion, he may not be the prettiest horse in the world, but there aren't many braver. For when he fought back to outclass Sea Pigeon up that final hill it was practically his second race of the day following his strenuous work-out in the morning."

Monksfield was due to fly home on Thursday morning but when it was discovered there were six mares on the plane he was switched to a later flight. The merest twinkle in his green eyes, Des McDonogh comments, "Apparently the airline people did not believe the rumour that Monkey is a fairy!" He returned home to an enthusiastic reception and a huge sign emblazoned across the door of his box, "I'm a Champ without a doubt. All you critics eat your hearts out."

There's no doubt at all that Monksfield was some way short of his peak form on the day he won the 1979 Waterford Crystal Champion Hurdle. His subsequent performances proved it beyond question and both his trainer and jockey are convinced that he improved considerably in the 17 days before he contested the Colt Sigma Hurdle (formerly the Templegate Hurdle) at Liverpool on March 31st.

Monksfield always carries a big tummy but after Cheltenham he became fitter still. His coat became progressively brighter until it was glistening and he was as hard as iron, bulging with muscle. A bit of warm spring weather made all the difference.

196

Michael and Sheila Mangan, extending their holiday in Dunmore, spent an afternoon with a close friend, Michael Walsh, then, on the spur of the moment, with a few more friends, took the magnificent Champion Hurdle trophy to the local convent church to offer a prayer of thanksgiving for such a famous victory.

The week after Cheltenham was also memorable at Billywood for the long overdue success of their most loyal supporter Felix McCabe with Off Target at Sligo, ridden by Frank Skelly. Felix had bought the horse as an unseen foal for only £125 from Helen's mother and had waited almost five years for this, his first win as an owner.

Monksfield, meanwhile, enjoyed a few days rest, cantered with renewed zeal and twice worked really well before setting off for Liverpool on Wednesday, March 28th with Stranfield and Lisdu. The authorities there had not been expecting such early visitors and Des McDonogh found, to his consternation, the racecourse stables entrance firmly sealed with nailed planks. Luckily Liverpool's Mr Fixit, of the dark glasses and bristling moustache, Mike Dillon, was on hand to open up the stables.

The same evening Des and another Irish trainer Tommy Lacy called at the Holiday Inn unaware that a party was being held there for the English and Liverpool football international Emlyn Hughes after his testimonial match earlier in the evening. Mike Dillon, inevitably, was at the thrash; spotting the two Irish trainers sitting rather disconsolately in the corner of a deserted bar, he asked Emlyn Hughes if they might join the party. Five minutes later Mike Dillon had once more lived up to his nickname since the Liverpool players, all racing enthusiasts, were delighted to meet Monksfield's trainer.

The evening progressed, Emlyn Hughes, Alan Hansen, Terry McDermott and Ray Clemence, in particular, spent hours talking racing with their two surprise guests, and Emlyn, with typical generosity, invited them along to Anfield the next day to see the ground, the trophy room and the players during a training session. Ginger McCain, Red Rum's trainer, was also at the party. He was hoping for a prominent showing in the Grand National from Wayward Scot, a horse he owned in partnership with Emlyn Hughes. Before leaving, Ginger invited Des and

Helen to his annual pre-National party on the Friday night. In addition Ray Clemence was able to use his considerable influence to help Des move to the hotel where he had stayed in the two previous years.

Des recalls, "Those days at Liverpool gave me a much needed holiday. The pressure was off and it was marvellous to meet all the Liverpool team. We were also introduced to the manager, Bob Paisley, and Tommy Lacy and I even ran out through the tunnel on to the Anfield pitch."

On the Thursday Stranfield, ridden by Tommy Kinane, started favourite for the Holiday Inn Handicap Hurdle but his lack of experience showed against older horses and he trailed in one from last behind Birds Nest. Sea Pigeon could have run in and won the race but Peter Easterby, obsessed perhaps with the idea of beating Monksfield, held him back for Saturday.

The McCains' National eve party on Friday night was an exuberant affair. Shortly before midnight we all trooped outside to see Red Rum, surely the greatest horse in the history of the Grand National. Ginger McCain's home is, in many ways, as unlikely a setting for an equine fairytale as Billywood Stud. Ginger and his wife Beryl live in a small house immediately behind his car sales forecourt in a quiet Southport street. Opposite is a Chinese take-away shop. A few yards to the left is a busy railway crossing gate. To find Red Rum you simply walk through the kitchen into the small yard and there, in the nearest box to the house, standing proudly, head erect, is the legend of Aintree. Winner of three Grand Nationals, second in two more, he retired on the eve of the 1977 race. Since then he has adapted contentedly to his new role as a superstar, earning vast fees for personal appearances. When he is resting between engagements Red Rum still leads the stable's string of horses through the tree-lined streets of suburbia to the chain harrowed gallop on the beach.

McCain, heavily-built, his face topped with a ginger thatch, shakes with laughter as he insists, "When Rummy comes out in the morning it's just like a scene from a western when the gunman appears on the street. He catjumps across the road, scattering passers-by, causing confusion as he careers along sideways."

198

For fully 10 minutes the McDonoghs stood in awe in his box. Des confirms, "I was mad keen to see him and was absolutely captivated. I'll remember it for the rest of my life. His character, in so many ways, was just like Monkey's. He obviously adored people, loved being looked at, and, of course, it's people that make horses. He was very vain, enjoyed being chatted up and given polo mints. What a fine horse with not a mark or blemish on his lower limbs after all that mileage. His coat was gleaming. Most of all I thought what a lucky man Ginger was to be able to keep such a close relationship with his horse in retirement."

On Saturday Monksfield was set to give 5 pounds to his three rivals, Sea Pigeon, Kybo and Western Rose in the Colt Sigma Hurdle over 2 miles, $5\frac{1}{2}$ furlongs. He had won the race for the past two years but many observers felt Sea Pigeon would reverse the Cheltenham form on much faster going and Kybo, travelling so smoothly when he fell in the Champion Hurdle, was strongly fancied by his stable to atone for that lapse. Early in the morning ante-post bookmakers were generous enough to offer 7/4 against Monksfield but these odds were soon snapped up and by the time of the race his price had shortened to 5/4 with Kybo and Sea Pigeon bracketed together at 5/2 and Western Rose ignored at 16/1. Monksfield simply outclassed and outstayed his opponents in a vintage performance that, on figures alone, must surely rate as the finest of his long and illustrious career.

His old friend Tommy Kinane, watching intently, insists, "Golden Cygnet, if he had been alive, would not have seen what way Monksfield was going at Liverpool. Golden Cygnet, Persian War, Hatton's Grace, all the great hurdlers put into one bag would not have beaten him that day. He was like a greyhound, the best I've ever seen him. Normally he only lets fly at the end of a race, you'll be push, push, shove and then suddenly he switches into a Rolls-Royce. But at Liverpool he was flying from the start, different class to the rest. I tell you I've had some enjoyment from riding that horse, *some enjoyment*. But that day was the greatest of his life."

Dessie Hughes, too, was effusive in his praise after the race but the first half mile gave him some anxious moments. He recalls, "I set off in the lead, jumped the first, and he felt stone cold under me, *empty*, there was nothing there. He was not even striding

199

Monksfield gallops away from Kybo (left) and Sea Pigeon (falling) at the final flight of the Colt Sigma Hurdle at Liverpool. *Credit: George Selwyn*

out. We jumped the second, and he was still the same, *lifeless*, dead under me. I was afraid I would have to give him a smack to wake him up, but I didn't because I feared something was terribly wrong. I jumped the third and it was no better. I was really worried. What was I to do? Then suddenly half-way round the first bend he came alive, picked up his bit, started pulling really strong. It was as if someone had given him a dig in the backside with a pig prodder. He just took off, put his toe out and was never going to be beaten. He was brilliant.''

Monksfield led for the first two miles before Dessie Hughes, as planned, gave him a breather, allowing Bob Champion to steal a lead of two or three lengths on Kybo turning for home for the final time. As Kybo came wide into the straight Monksfield switched back on to the far rail. It looked for a moment like a game of equine musical chairs as the four horses changed

200

urgently from line astern to jockeying frantically for positions but Monksfield stamped his authority on his rivals in a hundred yards when the race began in earnest. Two lengths behind Kybo at the third last hurdle, he sauntered back into the lead before the next jump and skipped over it with the race already won. On the run to the final hurdle Dessie Hughes allowed himself the rare luxury of a long, long look over his shoulder before pulling down his goggles. He explains, "Even though Monksfield was cruising I was wondering about Sea Pigeon. When you are in front, wearing goggles, it is very hard to see a horse coming until he's nearly on top of you. The steel reflectors on the sides shut off your vision. Without the goggles you'll see an extra half a length out of the corner of your eye."

Behind him Kybo was well beaten and Sea Pigeon several lengths adrift was struggling vainly to close the gap. Jonjo O'Neill remembers, "Dessie was looking round for so long I thought he wasn't going to see the last hurdle." Monksfield flew the final flight and galloped right away from Kybo but Sea Pigeon, running out of stamina, fell heavily and Jonjo walked back sadly to change for his ride on the favourite Alverton in the Grand National.

The McDonoghs, trapped in the vast crowd, missed the huge ovation given to Monksfield for winning the same race three years running.

Among Monksfield's more fervent, raucous supporters at Liverpool was a flamboyant character, Aidan O'Connell, about to have his first ride in the Grand National, on the 500/1 outsider Vindicate. O'Connell lives life to the full, something of a problem when you are trying to melt down your usual 14 stone to a sylph-like 11 stone in less than a month. Tall with sparkling eyes, a ruddy face, an immaculate dresser, a carnation always in his lapel Aidan O'Connell is that rare animal, an Irish dandy. On his arm at Liverpool was a lovely blonde, warm-eyed temptress whose attentions seemed to be straying towards some of the better known Grand National jockeys gathering nearby in their bright silks.

O'Connell told her sharply, "Jesus, if I had the time I'd sort you out." His delicious companion replied, coolly and truthfully, "If you had the money I would let you."

Turning to applaud Monksfield Aidan said, "He's the bravest horse you will ever see. A lot of people were giving out stink about the horse running too often in the wrong races, but Des assesses the horse superbly and brings him to his peak at the right time. To coast in like that at Liverpool after such a hard race at Cheltenham should have been impossible. I've never seen a braver horse and I wish I had one with an engine like him. If only I did a transplant with Vindicate I might have a chance in the National."

Vindicate's forlorn attempt ended abruptly when he fell at the first fence. The horse was uninjured but his colourful amateur rider was taken to hospital before discharging himself early in the evening because two doctors could not agree on their diagnosis of his shoulder injury. Later in the afternoon Helen, too, fell on Stranfield, brought down in a mêlée at the fifth hurdle. Stranfield was unhurt and Helen eventually struggled to her feet despite two painful kicks.

Monksfield's exploits at Cheltenham and Liverpool earned his trainer the Pommery and Greno award of champagne for the second March in succession. The Liverpool executive, too, were so impressed by the horse's popularity that they decided to name a race after him at the Grand National meeting in 1980. The Monksfield Hurdle, over 2 miles, $5\frac{1}{2}$ furlongs, will be run on the first day of the meeting just two days before the race he may well attempt to win for a fourth time.

Stranfield and Lisdu were sick horses by the time they returned to Billywood. Both had picked up the dreaded virus at Liverpool with the classic symptoms of cough, runny noses and temperatures. The disease spread swiftly through the yard but the one horse who seemed unaffected was Monksfield, despite the fact that the horse in the adjoining box coughed non-stop for two weeks.

On just one morning Monksfield, too, had a slightly runny nose but Des McDonogh, with some misgivings, decided to go ahead with his plan to send him over for the Welsh Champion Hurdle at Chepstow in mid-April. Des travelled with the horse and Joe Brady on Thursday and spent his spare time walking the hills of South Wales. Helen flew over on Saturday in time to join him for a brief visit to Lambourn, the lovely Berkshire village at the heart of jump racing. Only two horses opposed Monksfield at Chepstow on the Monday, Birds Nest, beaten out of sight in the Champion Hurdle but a winner since at Liverpool, and the rank 50/1 outsider Autoway, presumably left in to collect third prize money of £829. Monksfield was alone at the racecourse stables for four days until Autoway's arrival late on Sunday night. The dual champion worked well enough on the undulating gallops on the inside of the track but his trainer was a little anxious about running him while the rest of his stable was closed down by the virus. Possibly he was off colour. Quite probably the ground was firmer than he liked. Certainly he would have preferred more company in the preceding days. Whatever the reason Monksfield gave his supporters a nasty fright before landing odds of 2/7 by 1½ lengths from Birds Nest.

For a moment, as the unconsidered outsider Autoway led by a dozen lengths going to the final turn, we all wondered if his unknown jockey Mark Williams had slipped his two rivals. Certainly Andy Turnell on Birds Nest felt a little anxious. He admitted, "We'd gone such a good gallop I could not really believe Autoway could keep it up but way ahead I could see his rider sitting up his neck, oozing confidence."

Just as the large crowd stirred uneasily the leader tired rapidly and it was Monksfield who showed ahead of Birds Nest as they rose at the second last hurdle. Running to the final hurdle Monksfield was just over a length in front but now Andy Turnell decided to use his ace, his horse's one, swift, often deadly burst of acceleration. Birds Nest knifed up alongside Monksfield but immediately Dessie Hughes felt the game dual champion tighten under him to repel the challenge. It never really materialized because a disastrous blunder at the final hurdle cost Birds Nest his chance. Andy Turnell remembers thinking, "What a waste to fall when we had our opportunity of winning." Somehow Birds Nest did not fall but while he recovered Monksfield ran on strongly to win comfortably. An exhausted Autoway eventually struggled home a distance behind the leading pair. Monksfield came back to warm applause and was cheered again as he left the winner's enclosure to return to the box on the course he had occupied since Thursday.

Bob Turnell, trainer of Birds Nest, shook Des McDonogh's

hand and insisted, "It was a good performance by your horse to give my fellow 5 pounds." Dessie Hughes, meanwhile, reported that Monksfield had been unhappy on the undulating track and had become very unbalanced on the downhill stretches. Later in the directors' room one of the Stewards apologized to Des McDonogh for the fact that he had been more or less marooned in Chepstow for five days without a car. The trainer smiled as he replied, "The exercise on the hills was good for my health."

On the way to London Airport that night Dessie Hughes quietly spelled out one of Monksfield's finest qualities. Shaking his head in surprise as Andy Turnell, at the wheel, scythed skilfully at high speed through the endless Bank Holiday traffic, Dessie said, "I don't think I've ever ridden a horse that enjoys his racing so much. He just loves to compete."

Meanwhile the McDonoghs were struggling at Chepstow under a trio of awards. Monksfield's exploits had earned him the title of Domecq Sherry Racehorse of the Month of March, and copious amounts of sherry for his trainer, owner, jockey and head lad. In addition Des McDonogh had collected his Pommery champagne at a friendly reception during the afternoon. Monday's prize at Chepstow also included a fine set of china for Michael Mangan which had to be taken back to Billywood. Such are the problems of training a champion!

Monksfield returned to England three weeks later for his final race of a long campaign, but a distressing 26-hour-long outward journey almost certainly cost him a triumphant farewell. With automatic top weight of 12 stone, he was set to give lumps of weight all round in the £25,000 Royal Doulton Handicap Hurdle at Haydock on May 7th. The previous year he had just failed to concede 2 stone to Royal Gaye but this time his trainer was optimistic he would defy the handicapper. The horse, as we have seen, was in superb form and the going, when he finally arrived exhausted at Haydock on Sunday morning, was the most perfect he had encountered all season, but the journey had clearly left its mark on the hardy champion. Monksfield set off from Billywood at the crack of dawn on Saturday morning but when he arrived at the docks in Dublin the authorities refused permission for him to be loaded because the ferry's stabilizer had been seriously damaged. So he and Joe Brady spent a fruitless, boring

204

Des and Helen McDonogh in jaunty mood at Chepstow after collecting his award as Pommery Trainer of the Month of March for the second year running.

and wasteful day waiting at a nearby stud until they were able to board the next ferry late on Saturday evening.

Joe recalls, "You could see he was jaded all right when he got to Haydock. As usual he did not pass any remarks but it was obvious he was tired so I just took him for a short walk on Sunday." Rain started to fall that evening, softly at first, but then with increasing venom and continued through the night right up to the time of the race. Early that morning Des McDonogh rode Monksfield with a growing feeling of dismay, then returned to his hotel to announce dismally to his fellow travellers that the sloppy ground had ruined Monksfield's chance of victory.

The trainer, for once, was so nearly wrong. Despite the huge weight and the dreadful underfoot conditions Monksfield only

205

just failed to beat the Champion Hurdle third Beacon Light and battled on doggedly through the slush and mud to be second, so extending his imposing record of finishing in the first two in all his ten races in England.

On the run in he was steadily catching Beacon Light (receiving 13 pounds), and was only beaten by two rapidly diminishing lengths, but anyone standing down at the third last hurdle would have been astounded to learn he had finished in the first half dozen. Early in the straight, as the field quickened in the sloppy ground, Monksfield, looking about as happy as a limousine in a ploughed field, had dropped back from the leading group. All his immense qualities of character, determination and matchless spirit were needed as he fought back past several rivals. But Beacon Light had gone beyond recall.

Afterwards Dessie Hughes reported, "Monksfield swam with me for two miles. It was slushy, loose ground and he could never get a grip with his unusual action. He was well beaten turning for home but the best of the going was in the straight and he just plugged on. If the ground had stayed right I'm sure he would have won.

Des McDonogh, initially, was despondent. He recalls, "I felt sorry for the horse. He was a bit dejected, he knew perfectly well he had been beaten, but we knew it was not his fault. All through the race you could see he wanted to be up there but with his action he was merely scooping out the loose top surface and could not get a proper grip."

Monksfield's courageous defeat at Haydock was the first of his races taped by Jenny McNamee's new, expensive video machine. The recording was made at the start of a three-hour tape and her regulars have made it quite clear they will take their custom elsewhere if she so much as considers taping over it. The film of that marvellous, inspiring comeback against impossible odds is still requested on most nights of the week, and the most intense conversations in the lounge bar cease automatically when the hero of the village gallops into vision once more.

Second prize money of £7,047 at Haydock took Monksfield's total earnings in win and place money from sixty-seven races just past the astonishing figure of £121,000.

206

# 21

# Racehorse of
# the Year

Monksfield began his summer holiday while his owner and trainer debated whether to keep him in training for one more season. It was not an easy decision. Most owners, I suspect, tempted by the prospect of steady, lucrative earnings from a long career at stud, would have retired him immediately. Michael Mangan is not an excessively wealthy man but to his eternal credit his policy with Monksfield has never been affected by commercial motivation or financial consideration. The horse obviously retained the most aggressive appetite for racing so Michael Mangan chose the bold policy of going for a third victory in the Champion Hurdle in 1980, a feat achieved by only three horses, Hatton's Grace, Sir Ken and Persian War, since the race was first held in 1927. Just for the record in that time only four entire horses, apart from Monksfield, have won the race . . . Saucy Kit, Anzio, Eborneezer and Seneca.

The plan is that Monksfield will race perhaps twice more after the Champion Hurdle then retire to stud for the 1981 covering season. But should he win decisively at Cheltenham, then, who knows, his owner and trainer might be tempted to keep him in training for yet another year!

In mid-summer 1979 Des McDonogh upped his fees to £42 a week, still absurdly cheap by English standards and a further row of new boxes improved his capacity to more than thirty. Staff, too, had been increased. Three more lads had joined the stable, though one of them could not ride. Occasionally one or two of them failed to show up in the mornings, particularly at hay-making time. Plans to build a new house were shelved

Monksfield picks at hay from the Champion Hurdle Trophy.

through lack of funds. The money had been spent instead on modernizing, improving and increasing the stable yard so the McDonoghs settled for an extension to their cramped bungalow.

The absurdly long postal strike finally ended at the end of June. Much to the McDonoghs' chagrin the telephone began to ring again after months of silence but more pleasantly odd letters of congratulation, some posted in March, started to filter through to Billywood.

One writer began, "I've never written a letter like this before but to see Monksfield battling up the hill yesterday in such testing conditions brought the most enormous lump to my throat and I could not speak for 10 minutes after the race."

Another wrote, "I thought Crisp's Grand National was the highpoint of all race finishes along with Fred Winter's acrobatic ride on Mandarin in France with a broken bit, but I think Monksfield yesterday topped those races."

A letter of congratulation started simply, "Dear Monksfield" and a female admirer from England sent a £5 note to be spent on Monksfield's favourite Granny Smith apples, "as a small repayment for all the pleasure he has given me."

Robin Cutler, a bright young vet increasingly helping the stable, offered an intriguing reason for Monksfield's continuing success. "If you think of Monksfield in terms of a motor converting into speed going forward," he says, "then he is a very economical machine. His proportions are right and there is no spare weight at all on him. He is close to perfection, very short from the knee to the ground. The importance about his stride is the great length he stays in the air and that means he goes faster, using less energy. In addition intelligence and ability must be related. He loves a challenge."

A welcome visitor in June was Paddy Broderick, still not fully recovered from that dreadful fall with Night Nurse in December 1977. Paddy arrived on holiday from his home at Bishop Auckland with his wife Nancy and their 9-year-old daughter Alison, already an accomplished rider in gymkhanas.

Sea Pigeon, meanwhile, recovered from that shaking fall at Liverpool, finished second to Birds Nest in the Scottish Champion Hurdle. At the ripe old age of 9 he proceeded to show improved form yet again on the flat, for in one hectic month in mid-season he won the £10,000 Tennent Trophy at Ayr and then added surely his greatest triumph of all, one of the most competitive handicaps, the Tote-Ebor at York in mid-August again under top weight, ridden for the first time on the flat by Jonjo O'Neill.

Will he be back for another crack at Monksfield in March 1980? "Certainly," says his owner Pat Muldoon. "As a spectacle what could possibly be better than a repeat of the 1979 race? At the last hurdle Sea Pigeon seemed certain to win but the little horse outstayed him on the hill in the heavy conditions. If we don't run Sea Pigeon then Monksfield will start at long odds-on. He has matchless courage and durability but I just wish we could meet him in a flat race. Sea Pigeon would certainly pick him up then, he has so much more speed."

Whatever the result of the 1980 Champion Hurdle Sea Pigeon's eventual task will be as a schoolmaster for Pat

Muldoon's son Stephen, who will be 16 in February 1980. Their joint target is to win the 1 mile, 7 furlongs amateur riders race on the opening day of the Ayr Western meeting late in the year.

Peter Ryan, whose lucky trip to Dublin started the Monksfield fairytale, has always been listed, quite correctly, as the horse's breeder. In the summer of 1979 Arthur Ryan asked Peter if his name might be added, officially, as joint breeder. Peter readily agreed. He explains, "As far as I am concerned Arthur is a full partner. I was keen to amend the records to make him joint breeder." Peter wrote to the Turf Club in Dublin, but, perhaps because of the long postal strike, did not receive a reply. Eventually he asked the Jockey Club for advice and was told, quite firmly, that he must remain the sole breeder of Monksfield. The rule, it was explained, stated quite clearly that the owner of a mare at the time a foal drops is, by definition, the breeder. There was not the slightest possibility of an exception being made in the case of Monksfield.

Since the birth of Regina's Way, Regina has been barren to Gala Performance, Al Sarat and Lucifer. In 1979 at the age of 22 she retired to the fields of Inch and, when the time comes, will be put down quietly and painlessly and buried in the big field where she once ran with her famous offspring.

Tommy Kinane's pain at losing the ride on Monksfield had at last eased. He says, "Des and I have both been hot-headed at times but we are still in the game together and have to live. I don't hold grudges, life's too short for that." Tommy's attitude has, no doubt, been mellowed by his own experiences as a trainer dealing with difficult situations. He admits, "I see the problems all right, I'm not blind. Some owners buy a horse, send it to you and expect it to have five gears straight away. They might end up with a horse with one gear and that a slow one. I tell you one thing; I put a fellow out of here with his three horses as quick as lightning. I'll do it again if I have to; I'd rather have an empty stable than a bad tenant."

His eyes narrow as he adds, "I've not given up hope of winning the 1980 Champion Hurdle on Monksfield, maybe, or Stranfield, or even Monaco Prince. I'll be back, be sure of that. How long will I go on riding? People have been asking me that question for 10 years ... never mind this year. Don't worry,

210

I have no intention of giving up for some time to come. I'm not finished yet," he concludes defiantly.

All the considerable hidden pressures of training had not blunted Des McDonogh's quick-witted humour. Discussing an owner who was always late paying his bills Des said, "I wouldn't mind but if he stood on his money he would reach the moon."

By the autumn of 1979 Des McDonogh had trained fifty-two winners in almost seven years, exactly half of them owned by Michael Mangan; Monksfield had contributed eighteen victories, the faithful Kavala seven and Gatelle one. Now Dr Mangan owns a promising young colt Lavylaroe, bought cheaply for 2,600 guineas. A new, highly promising Cheltenham prospect joined the yard in the late autumn, Mister Niall, talented enough on the flat to finish third in the 1979 Irish 2,000 Guineas.

The Racehorse of the Year dinner, held appropriately enough

Des McDonogh and his youngest daughter Ashling in the stable yard. *Credit: Colm Farren*

on the final day of the English jump season, added yet another honour to Monksfield. He, of course, was elsewhere, catching up with a little peace and relaxation in a green field close to his trainer's bungalow. Dessie Hughes, too, was missing, after a dreadful fall the previous evening on Beparoejojo in which he broke his leg for the third time in two years, and also his arm and chestbone. The Mangans flew over for the festive weekend from Newfoundland and the McDonoghs conjured up enough petrol from their friendly local dealer to drive to Dublin airport for the flight to England. Guests gathered at the Stratford Hilton Hotel that night to honour the two champion racehorses of the year, Shirley Heights, the 1978 dual Derby winner and Monksfield, who had polled the highest number of votes since Arkle 12 years earlier – the only two Irish jumpers ever to be chosen. The most popular item on the menu was the film show that coincided with the brandy and coffee.

As the cigar smoke curled into the warm summer air in the packed dining-room shortly before midnight the guests, enthralled, watched again two of the finest races in the previous 12 months. The contrast between their reception was perhaps more a comment on the delicate balance between the jumping fans, who had just spent two enjoyable days racing at Stratford, and the various flat racing enthusiasts who had arrived in the last 24 hours. Whatever the reason Shirley Heights' thrilling late victory burst was greeted merely with a murmur of polite applause as the lights came on again. Monksfield, however, was cheered and roared on with lusty cries of encouragement as he and Sea Pigeon joined battle once more on the muddy slopes of Cheltenham. When it became apparent he would catch and pass Sea Pigeon, the dinner jacketed audience burst into a loud and spontaneous ovation.

Des McDonogh, sitting a little uneasily at the top table, sipped his umpteenth soft drink of the night and confided later, "It was worth coming all this way just to hear that reception. Sometimes I feel people over here appreciate Monkey more than in his own country."

Michael Mangan, pausing to brush back a lock of grey hair, removed his dark glasses before beginning an emotional and at times amusing speech of thanks, ending with a stanza from Paul

212

Mellon's Gimcrack poem that might have been written specifically for Monksfield.

> "Swift as a bird I flew down many a course,
> Princes, Lords, Commoners all sang my praise.
> In victory or defeat I played my part.
> Remember me, all men who love the Horse,
> If hearts and spirits flag in after days;
> Though small, I gave my all. I gave my heart."

# Racing Record

## FLAT RACING

### 1974

Punchestown. October 23rd. Yielding
Elverstown Maiden Plate (Div II). 7 furlongs, 110 yards. £517.50

| | | | | |
|---|---|---|---|---|
| Monksfield | 2–9–0 | K. Coogan | 25–1 | 1 |
| Matisse | 2–9–0 | C. Roche | 5–4 Fav | 2 |
| Ardallen | 2–9–0 | D. Hogan | 3–1 | 3 |

14 ran. Distances: ¾l, 1l

### 1975

Navan. April 9th. Good
Sloppy Weather Plate. 1 mile, 2 furlongs. £276

| | | | | |
|---|---|---|---|---|
| Ardallen | 3–9–0 | D. Hogan | 7–4 Fav | 1 |
| Say Cheese | 3–8–10 | C. Seward | 3–1 | 2 |
| Monksfield | 3–9–0 | K. Coogan | 6–1 | 3 |

25 ran. Distances: 1l, 1½l. Trained S. Quirke

Leopardstown. April 23rd. Good
Rockbrook Stakes. 7 furlongs    Unplaced (seventh of eleven)

The Curragh. May 16th. Yielding
Royal Whip Stakes. 1½ miles    Unplaced (seventh of nine)

Dundalk. May 23rd. Firm
Blackrock Handicap. 1½ miles       Unplaced (ninth of twelve)


Leopardstown. June 2nd. Good
Loughlinstown Ladies' Plate. 1¾ miles. £483

| | | | | |
|---|---|---|---|---|
| Sunbeam Princess | 3–8–4 | Miss E. Carmody | 10–1 | 1 |
| Monksfield | 3–9–3 | Mrs D. McDonogh | 3–1 | 2 |
| Starbands | 5–10–1 | Miss L. Cooper | 33–1 | 3 |

12 ran. Distances: 6l, 1l. Trained L. Browne


The Curragh. June 7th. Firm
Lone Bush Stakes. 1¾ miles       Unplaced (eighth of thirteen)


The Curragh. September 20th. Good
October Handicap. 1½ miles       Unplaced (eleventh of twelve)


Leopardstown. September 27th. Good
Harvester Handicap. 1¾ miles       Unplaced (fifth of fourteen)
Subsequently disqualified and placed last when rider failed to weigh-in.


Navan. October 1st. Good
Tara Maiden Plate. 1¼ miles       Unplaced (fifth of eight)


Naas. October 11th. Firm
Blessington Handicap. 1½ miles       Unplaced (ninth of eleven)


The Curragh. October 18th. Yielding
Irish Cesarewitch. 2 miles. £3,158.50

| | | | | |
|---|---|---|---|---|
| Prominent King | 3–8–2 | P. Martin | 14–1 | 1 |
| Oranmore | 5–8–0 | J. Roe | 33–1 | 2 |
| Monksfield | 3–7–2 | S. Craine | 33–1 | 3 |

21 ran. Distances: 2½l, ¾l. Trained K. Prendergast


The Curragh. November 1st. Soft
J. T. Rogers Memorial Gold Cup Handicap. 2 miles
      Unplaced (ninth of twenty-one)


Naas. November 8th. Good
Naas November Handicap. 1½ miles
      Unplaced (sixth of twenty-one)

215

## 1976

Naas. April 10th. Good
Halverstown Apprentice Plate (Div II). 1½ miles. £483

| Monksfield | 4–8–0 | M. J. Kinane | 8–1 | 1 |
| Masqued Dancer | 4–9–3 | T. Carmody | 4–6 Fav | 2 |
| Cnoch Bhui | 4–8–6 | B. Coogan | 3–1 | 3 |

15 ran. Distances: Head, 2½l

The Curragh. October 16th. Yielding
Irish Cesarewitch. 2 miles
Unplaced (not in first nine of twenty-nine)

The Curragh. October 30th. Soft
J. T. Rogers Memorial Gold Cup Handicap. 2 miles
Unplaced (eighth of twenty-three)

Naas. November 6th. Good
Naas November Handicap. 1½ miles
Unplaced (not in first nine of twenty-six)

## 1977

Naas. April 16th. Good
Halverstown Apprentice Plate. 1½ miles. £483

| Monksfield | 5–8–13 | M. J. Kinane | 5–2 Fav | 1 |
| Majetta Crescent | 4–8–11 | Miss Joanna Morgan | 3–1 | 2 |
| Wonder Gleam | 4–8–6 | T. Maskell | 14–1 | 3 |

25 ran. Distances: 1l, 1½l

The Curragh. October 15th. Good
Irish Cesarewitch. 2 miles
Unplaced (not in first nine of twenty-eight)

The Curragh. October 29th. Soft
J. T. Rogers Memorial Gold Cup Handicap. 2 miles. £1,572.60

| Mr Kildare | 4–10–3 | T. Carmody | 12–1 | 1 |
| La Cita | 3–7–12 | B. Coogan | 6–1 | 2 |
| Monksfield | 5–8–12 | P. Sullivan | 14–1 | 3 |

21 ran. Distances: ½l, 4l. Trained L. Browne

Leopardstown. November 12th. Soft
Leopardstown November Handicap. 2 miles
Unplaced (ninth of twenty-two)

1978

Naas. April 15th. Good
Halverstown Apprentice Plate (Div I). 1½ miles. £483

| | | | | |
|---|---|---|---|---|
| Monksfield | 6–9–2 | M. J. Kinane | 8–11 Fav | 1 |
| Rare Talk | 4–7–13 | D. Byrne | 12–1 | 2 |
| Timur | 5–8–10 | B. Coogan | 25–1 | 3 |

13 ran. Distances: 4l, Short Head

Leopardstown. April 19th. Good
Savel Beg Stakes. 2 miles. £3,064

| | | | | |
|---|---|---|---|---|
| Monksfield | 6–9–13 | D. T. Hughes | 3–1 Jt Fav | 1 |
| Rathinree | 5–9–13 | T. Murphy | 3–1 Jt Fav | 2 |
| La Valencia | 5–9–0 | Miss Joanna Morgan | 33–1 | 3 |

22 ran. Distances: 1½l, Short Head

The Curragh. October 7th. Good
Irish Cesarewitch. 2 miles

Unplaced (not in first nine of twenty-three)

The Curragh. October 28th. Good
J. T. Rogers Memorial Gold Cup Handicap. 2 miles

Unplaced (ninth of sixteen)

## HURDLE RACING

1975–76

Navan. November 22nd. Good
Tara Maiden Hurdle (Div II). 3-year-olds. 2 miles. £915.40

| | | | | |
|---|---|---|---|---|
| Monksfield | 10–11 | R. Coonan | 5–1 | 1 |
| Almanac | 10–11 | P. Colville | 8–1 | 2 |
| Swift Flyer | 10–11 | J. J. Gallagher | 6–1 | 3 |

22 ran. Distances: 1½l, 8l

Fairyhouse. December 6th. Yielding
Ashbourne Hurdle (Div I). 3-year-olds. 2 miles. £690

| | | | | |
|---|---|---|---|---|
| Monksfield | 11–5 | F. Berry | 7–1 | 1 |
| Troyswood | 11–5 | T. Carberry | 5–4 Fav | 2 |
| King Weasel | 11–5 | R. Coonan | 5–2 | 3 |

24 ran. Distances: 4l, ¾l

Leopardstown. December 26th. Good
Three-Year-Old Hurdle (Div II). 2 miles

Unplaced (ninth of fifteen)


Navan. January 17th. Good
Proudstown Handicap Hurdle. 2 miles

Unplaced (fourth of fourteen)


Naas. January 24th. Good
Celbridge Handicap Hurdle. 2 miles, 1 furlong. £1,649.50

| | | | | |
|---|---|---|---|---|
| Straight Row | 6–11–2 | T. Carberry | 100–30 | 1 |
| Monksfield | 4–9–7 | T. Kinane | 8–1 | 2 |
| Irish Fashion | 5–10–12 | T. McGivern | 11–4 Fav | 3 |

10 ran. Distances: Head, 4l. Trained J. Dreaper


Navan. February 11th. Soft
Tara Handicap Hurdle. 2 miles          Unplaced (fifth of fifteen)


Fairyhouse. February 21st. Yielding
Monaloe Handicap Hurdle. 2 miles. £1,035

| | | | | |
|---|---|---|---|---|
| Bedwell Prince | 5–9–4 | E. McDonald | 12–1 | 1 |
| Monksfield | 4–9–12 | T. Kinane | 9–2 Fav | 2 |
| Ballymountain Girl | 7–10–2 | R. Hendrick | 14–1 | 3 |

17 ran. Distances: Head, 8l. Trained D. L. Moore


Navan. March 6th. Good
Beechmount Handicap Hurdle. 2 miles. £1,104

| | | | | |
|---|---|---|---|---|
| Monksfield | 4–10–7 | T. Kinane | 3–1 | 1 |
| Notary | 4–10–0 | T. Carberry | 5–2 Fav | 2 |
| Gladden | 5–10–13 | G. Newman | 8–1 | 3 |

11 ran. Distances: ¾l, ¾l


Cheltenham. March 18th. Firm
*Daily Express* Triumph Hurdle. 4-year-olds. 2 miles, 200 yards.
£9,591.50

| | | | | |
|---|---|---|---|---|
| Peterhof | 11–0 | J. J. O'Neill | 10–1 | 1 |
| Monksfield | 11–0 | T. Kinane | 28–1 | 2 |
| Prominent King | 11–0 | F. Berry | 4–1 Fav | 3 |

23 ran. Distances: 1½l, Neck. Trained M. W. Easterby. Objection to
winner by second overruled

Fairyhouse. April 21st. Good
Huzzar Handicap Hurdle. 2 miles. £3,649

| | | | | |
|---|---|---|---|---|
| Monksfield | 4–9–9 | T. Kinane | 4–1 Jt Fav | 1 |
| Bedwell Prince | 5–9–7 | E. McDonald | 14–1 | 2 |
| Hunters Gift | 4–9–7 | A. C. Brennan | 33–1 | 3 |

16 ran. Distances: 8l, Short Head


Punchestown. April 28th. Firm
Downshire Handicap Hurdle. 2 miles. £2,588

| | | | | |
|---|---|---|---|---|
| Multiple | 6–10–0 | T. J. Kinane (Jun) | 12–1 | 1 |
| Rostan | 8–10–10 | F. Berry | 5–1 | 2 |
| Monksfield | 4–11–7 | T. Kinane | 7–4 Fav | 3 |

10 ran. Distances: Head, 3l. Trained C. Kinane


1976–77

Punchestown. October 20th. Good
Free Handicap Hurdle. 2 miles. £1,698.50

| | | | | |
|---|---|---|---|---|
| Dublin Express | 5–10–6 | C. Seward | 16–1 | 1 |
| Friendliness | 4–9–10 | T. Carmody | 20–1 | 2 |
| Monksfield | 4–11–3 | R. Coonan | 3–1 | 3 |

9 ran. Distances: 3l, ½l. Trained M. O'Toole


Navan. November 20th. Good
Dunsany Handicap Hurdle. 2 miles. £963

| | | | | |
|---|---|---|---|---|
| What a Slave | 5–9–12 | M. Morris | 5–2 Fav | 1 |
| Call The Tune | 6–10–7 | T. Carmody | 20–1 | 2 |
| Monksfield | 4–11–5 | T. Kinane | 9–2 | 3 |

14 ran. Distances: 3l, Short Head. Trained J. B. Lusk


Naas. November 27th. Good
Naas Handicap Hurdle. 2 miles, 3 furlongs

Unplaced (tenth of eighteen)


Fairyhouse. December 4th. Soft
Irish Benson & Hedges Handicap Hurdle. 2 miles. £3,579

| | | | | |
|---|---|---|---|---|
| Monksfield | 4–11–4 | T. Kinane | 7–1 | 1 |
| Ballymountain Girl | 7–10–1 | G. Newman | 16–1 | 2 |
| Straight Row | 6–11–7 | M. Cummins | 10–1 | 3 |

16 ran. Distances: 2l, 2½l

219

Leopardstown. December 28th. Yielding
Sweeps Handicap Hurdle. 2 miles. £12,457.50

| | | | | |
|---|---|---|---|---|
| Master Monday | 6–10–2 | J. Harty | 25–1 | 1 |
| Straight Row | 6–10–13 | T. Carberry | 6–1 | 2 |
| Dublin Express | 5–10–5 | R. Townend | 25–1 | 3 |
| Monksfield | 4–11–0 | T. Kinane | 9–1 | 4 |

19 ran. Distances: 2½l, 8l, 2l. Trained L. Quirke

Naas. January 22nd. Soft
Celbridge Handicap Hurdle. 2 miles, 3 furlongs. £1,810.50

| | | | | |
|---|---|---|---|---|
| Fish Quiz | 6–12–0 | M. Cummins | 7–1 | 1 |
| Fanfare Beauty | 6–9–2 | S. Kemble | 20–1 | 2 |
| Cytisus | 6–10–1 | P. Gill | 20–1 | 3 |
| Monksfield | 5–11–10 | T. Kinane | 8–1 | 4 |

14 ran. Distances: ¾l, 6l, Short Head. Trained J. Dreaper

Navan. January 24th. Soft
Proudstown Handicap Hurdle. 2 miles. £1,364

| | | | | |
|---|---|---|---|---|
| Monksfield | 5–12–0 | T. Kinane | 8–1 | 1 |
| Director General | 7–9–6 | S. Kemble | 4–1 | 2 |
| Poll's Turn | 6–10–5 | F. Berry | 7–2 Fav | 3 |

13 ran. Distances: 2½l, 3l

Fairyhouse. February 12th. Heavy
Monaloe Handicap Hurdle. 2 miles, 2 furlongs

Unplaced (fifth of eleven)

Leopardstown. February 19th. Heavy
Erin Foods Champion Hurdle. 2 miles. £8,881

| | | | | |
|---|---|---|---|---|
| Master Monday | 7–12–0 | J. Harty | 20–1 | 1 |
| Comedy of Errors | 10–12–0 | J. Burke | 13–8 Fav | 2 |
| Monksfield | 5–11–11 | T. Kinane | 8–1 | 3 |

16 ran. Distances: 4l, 1½l. Trained L. Quirke

Navan. March 5th. Soft
Beechmount Hotel Handicap Hurdle. 2 miles. £1,104

| | | | | |
|---|---|---|---|---|
| Ballymountain Girl | 8–10–0 | R. Hendrick | 8–1 | 1 |
| Chinrullah | 5–9–1 | T. Maskell | 100–30 Fav | 2 |
| Monksfield | 5–12–0 | T. Kinane | 5–1 | 3 |

17 ran. Distances: Head, 2½l. Trained T. Walsh

Cheltenham. March 16th. Heavy
Champion Hurdle Challenge Cup. 2 miles, 200 yards. £18,147.50

| | | | | |
|---|---|---|---|---|
| Night Nurse | 6–12–0 | P. Broderick | 15–2 | 1 |
| Monksfield | 5–12–0 | T. Kinane | 15–1 | 2 |
| Dramatist | 6–12–0 | W. Smith | 6–1 | 3 |

10 ran. Distances: 2l, 2l. Trained M. H. Easterby

Liverpool. April 2nd. Firm
Templegate Hurdle. 2 miles, 5½ furlongs. £4,799.75 to each Dead
Heater

| | | | | |
|---|---|---|---|---|
| Monksfield | 5–11–5 | D. T. Hughes | 7–2 | 1 |
| Night Nurse | 6–11–11 | P. Broderick | 4–5 Fav | 1 |
| Peterhof | 5–11–5 | T. Stack | 10–1 | 3 |

10 ran. Distances: Dead Heat, 15l

Punchestown. April 27th. Soft
Downshire Handicap Hurdle. 2 miles. £2,798

| | | | | |
|---|---|---|---|---|
| Prince Tammy | 5–9–8 | P. Daly | 25–1 | 1 |
| Mwanadike | 5–11–2 | F. Berry | 6–1 | 2 |
| Troyswood | 5–10–9 | S. Treacy | 10–1 | 3 |
| Monksfield | 5–12–4 | D. T. Hughes | 7–1 | 4 |

18 ran. Distances: ½l, ½l, ¾l. Trained P. Mullins

## 1977–78

Punchestown. October 19th. Good
Free Handicap Hurdle. 2 miles          Unplaced (sixth of eight)

Leopardstown. October 31st. Soft
Squash Ireland Handicap Hurdle. 2 miles. £2,735

| | | | | |
|---|---|---|---|---|
| Meladon | 4–10–6 | T. Carberry | 4–5 Fav | 1 |
| Lovely Bio | 5–9–7 | T. Kinane | 9–2 | 2 |
| Monksfield | 5–12–2 | D. T. Hughes | 6–1 | 3 |

9 ran. Distances: 1l, 6l. Trained A. Maxwell

Down Royal. November 5th. Yielding
Name of the Game Trial Hurdle. 2 miles. £1,035

| | | | | |
|---|---|---|---|---|
| Flashy Boy | 9–10–11 | T. McGivern | 8–1 | 1 |
| Double Default | 7–11–0 | Mr C. Magnier | 8–1 | 2 |
| Monksfield | 5–11–10 | D. T. Hughes | 1–3 Fav | 3 |

7 ran. Distances: 6l, 1½l. Trained A. Watson

Navan. January 21st. Soft
Proudstown Handicap Hurdle. 2 miles          Unplaced (sixth of eight)

221

Leopardstown. February 18th. Yielding
Erin Foods Champion Hurdle. 2 miles. £9,010
| | | | | |
|---|---|---|---|---|
| Prominent King | 6–11–4 | R. Coonan | 6–1 | 1 |
| Mr Kildare | 5–11–1 | T. Carmody | 5–1 | 2 |
| Monksfield | 6–11–8 | T. Kinane | 11–1 | 3 |

16 ran. Distances: 2½l, 1l. Trained K. Prendergast

Cheltenham. March 15th. Good
Waterford Crystal Champion Hurdle Challenge Trophy. 2 miles,
200 yards. £21,332.50
| | | | | |
|---|---|---|---|---|
| Monksfield | 6–12–0 | T. Kinane | 11–2 | 1 |
| Sea Pigeon | 8–12–0 | F. Berry | 5–1 | 2 |
| Night Nurse | 7–12–0 | C. Tinkler | 3–1 Fav | 3 |

13 ran. Distances: 2l, 6l

Liverpool. April 1st. Firm
Templegate Hurdle. 2 miles, 5½ furlongs. £7,253.75
| | | | | |
|---|---|---|---|---|
| Monksfield | 6–11–11 | D. T. Hughes | 9–4 | 1 |
| Night Nurse | 7–11–6 | J. J. O'Neill | 13–8 Fav | 2 |
| Kybo | 5–11–5 | R. Champion | 18–1 | 3 |

7 ran. Distances: 2l, 10l

Haydock. May 1st. Firm
Royal Doulton Handicap Hurdle. 2 miles. £20,085.25
| | | | | |
|---|---|---|---|---|
| Royal Gaye | 5–10–0 | C. Tinkler | 20–1 | 1 |
| Monksfield | 6–12–0 | D. T. Hughes | 100–30 | 2 |
| Night Nurse | 7–11–9 | I. Watkinson | 8–1 | 3 |

20 ran. Distances: ¾l, 2½l. Trained F. Rimell

1978–79

Down Royal. November 4th. Good
A. R. Soudavar Memorial Trial Hurdle. 2 miles. £1,380
| | | | | |
|---|---|---|---|---|
| Monksfield | 6–11–10 | T. Kinane | Evens Fav | 1 |
| Double Default | 8–11–0 | Mr C. Magnier | 6–1 | 2 |
| Oisin Dubh | 6–11–10 | Mr M. Grassick | 16–1 | 3 |

7 ran. Distances: ¾l, 8l

Naas. November 25th. Yielding
Naas Handicap Hurdle. 2 miles, 3 furlongs. £2,693

| | | | | |
|---|---|---|---|---|
| Milan Major | 6–9–8 | P. Gill | 20–1 | 1 |
| Monksfield | 6–12–4 | T. Kinane | 9–2 | 2 |
| Troyswood | 6–10–5 | S. Treacy | 11–4 | 3 |

10 ran. Distances: 12l, Short Head. Trained T. Bergin

Fairyhouse. December 2nd. Soft
Benson and Hedges Handicap Hurdle. 2 miles. £8,540

| | | | | |
|---|---|---|---|---|
| Rathinree | 5–10–3 | T. McGivern | 9–4 Fav | 1 |
| Monksfield | 6–12–0 | T. Kinane | 11–2 | 2 |
| Troyswood | 6–10–0 | S. Treacy | 14–1 | 3 |

10 ran. Distances: 1½l, 1½l. Trained G. Armstrong

Leopardstown. December 27th. Heavy
Sweeps Handicap Hurdle. 2 miles. £11,476.50

| | | | | |
|---|---|---|---|---|
| Chinrullah | 6–10–6 | G. Newman | 8–1 | 1 |
| Glassilaun | 6–10–0 | T. J. Ryan | 14–1 | 2 |
| Monksfield | 6–12–0 | T. Kinane | 4–1 | 3 |

12 ran. Distances: 4l, 5l. Trained M. O'Toole

Leopardstown. February 24th. Yielding
Erin Foods Champion Hurdle. 2 miles        Unplaced (sixth of eight)

Cheltenham. March 14th. Heavy
Waterford Crystal Championship Hurdle Challenge Trophy. 2 miles, 200 yards. £22,730

| | | | | |
|---|---|---|---|---|
| Monksfield | 7–12–0 | D. T. Hughes | 9–4 Fav | 1 |
| Sea Pigeon | 9–12–0 | J. J. O'Neill | 6–1 | 2 |
| Beacon Light | 8–12–0 | J. Francome | 22–1 | 3 |

10 ran. Distances: ¾l, 15l

Liverpool. March 31st. Yielding
Colt Sigma Hurdle. 2 miles, 5½ furlongs. £8,597

| | | | | |
|---|---|---|---|---|
| Monksfield | 7–11–11 | D. T. Hughes | 5–4 Fav | 1 |
| Kybo | 6–11–6 | R. Champion | 5–2 | 2 |
| Western Rose | 7–11–6 | C. Tinkler | 16–1 | 3 |

4 ran. Distances: 8l, 15l

Chepstow. April 16th. Good
Welsh Champion Hurdle. 2 miles. £6,286.50

| | | | | |
|---|---|---|---|---|
| Monksfield | 7–12–0 | D. T. Hughes | 2–7 Fav | 1 |
| Birds Nest | 9–11–9 | A. Turnell | 3–1 | 2 |
| Autoway | 6–11–9 | M. Williams | 50–1 | 3 |

3 ran. Distances: 1½l, distance


Haydock. May 7th. Soft
Royal Doulton Handicap Hurdle. 2 miles. £23,127.75

| | | | | |
|---|---|---|---|---|
| Beacon Light | 8–11–1 | A. Turnell | 12–1 | 1 |
| Monksfield | 7–12–0 | D. T. Hughes | 6–4 Fav | 2 |
| Mayhem | 6–9–10 | Mr D. Oldham | 20–1 | 3 |

17 ran. Distances: 2l, ¾l. Trained R. Turnell